Job design and industrial democracy

'A hopeless attempt to see things whole is at least as
worthy as the equally hopeless task of isolating frag-
ments for study – and much more interesting.'

Joseph W. Meeker, *The Comedy of Survival*, New
York: Scribner, 1974.

International series on the quality of working life

Vol. 3

Editor-in-Chief

Hans van Beinum,
Foundation for Business Administration, Delft-Rotterdam

Editorial Panel

Fred Emery,
Australian National University, Canberra
Nitish R. De,
National Labour Institute, New Delhi
Mauk Mulder,
Foundation for Business Administration, Delft-Rotterdam
Einar Thorsrud,
Work Research Institutes, Oslo
Eric Trist,
University of Pennsylvania, Philadelphia
Dick Walton,
Harvard University, Boston
Tommy Wilson,
London Graduate School of Business Studies, London

Job design and industrial democracy

The case of Norway

Joep F. Bolweg
Institute for Personnel Management, Tilburg

Martinus Nijhoff Social Sciences Division
Leiden 1976

ISBN 90 207 0634 9

Printed by Mennen, Asten, the Netherlands.

Preface

The organization of work is under critique in many industrialized countries. Bureaucracy, specialization, repetitive technology, and hierarchical control structures are criticized by politicians, trade unionists, and social scientists. They argue for improved quality of work, for work democratization, and for the humanization of work. This book evaluates Norwegian field experiments in the area of job redesign which started already in 1964. Norway has therefore a lead in experience compared to most other countries, particularly to the United States, where debates and subsequent experiments revolving around the quality of working life and the democratization of work started only in the early seventies. The Norwegian social scientists who left their academic bastions and started action research drew heavily upon the 'open socio-technical system' thinking as developed by the Tavistock Institute of Human Relations in London. This descriptive evaluation study analyzes the job redesign experiments from an industrial democracy perspective and places the experiments in their national political and labor relations contexts. Special emphasis is given to the actual and potential role trade unions can play in shopfloor job design projects. The industrial relations system of the United States is generally used as reference point in this study.

The theory guiding the experiments regards work democratization through job redesign as a first step in a bottom-up process of organizational democratization. This book and similar analyses of experiments in Sweden, Denmark, The Netherlands, and the United States clearly suggest that shopfloor democratization is hardly possible in a hierarchically controlled organization if top management does not create adequate room to maneuver at the base of the organization. The logic of organizational hierarchy runs counter against the logic of a bottom-up democratization strategy. Our current understanding leads to the conclusion that higher organizational levels will have to re-define their power in order to make democratization at the shopfloor possible. Local unions have an important role to play in establishing the conditions which are necessary for job redesign to contribute to industrial democracy. A 'package approach' towards industrial democracy is presented with as main thesis the mutual supportive roles of representative and participative democratization methods in democratization processes. The Norwegian industrial relations system is analyzed according to this line of thought.

For me, this book represents the summation and integration of five years of thinking and research. Naturally many people helped with my research and influenced my thinking during this time. I am in particular indebted to the friendly staff of the Work Research Institutes in Oslo and to Jack Barbash of the University of Wisconsin. Barbash's thinking and stimulation have not only greatly influenced this study, but in fact he and Mike Aiken, also of the University of Wisconsin, made it possible for this study to emerge in its current descriptive form.

Joep F. Bolweg

Contents

Glossary

AFI = Arbeidsforsknings Instituttene (Work Research Institutes, Oslo).

DNA = Det Norske Arbeiderparti (Norwegian Labor party, the social democratic party with close ties to the labor unions).

EEC = European Economic Community.

HAF = Herøya Arbeider Forening (local trade union at Norsk Hydro's Herøya complex).

ILO = International Labor Organization (Geneva).

LO = Landsorganisasjonen (Norwegian Federation of Trade Unions).

NAF = Norsk Arbeidsgiver Forening (Norwegian Employer's Federation).

OECD = Organization for Economic Cooperation and Development (Paris).

SV = Socialistisk Valgforbund (Left Wing Socialist Front).

TCO = Tjanstemmanens Centralorganisation (Central Organization of Salaried Employees, Sweden).

NOTE: The bibliography consists of two parts. The first part contains sources in English, the second section includes all non-English, predominantly Norwegian, references. The latter references are indicated in the text by an asterisk, e.g. Gulowsen, 1971*, and are translated by the author unless otherwise noted.

1. Introduction to Norway and its industrial relations system[1]

OVERVIEW
Economic and social history – the late industrialization process – LO – NAF – the Basic Agreement – the peaceful industrial relations climate – current issues – cooperation a major characteristic.

Norway is a country with democratic traditions which can be traced back to the middle ages. The peasants in Scandinavia were never subject to a feudal system which so clearly left its marks on later developments in other European countries. The small amount of soil that can be cultivated did not provide a basis for the development of a rich and strong Norwegian landowning elite (Bull, 1956). As early as 1750 farmers in Sweden gathered for meetings resembling a modern parliament. Farmer representatives were consulted by kings on major decisions, like the implementation of new taxation systems. Of course the number of persons who participated in such meetings was highly restricted, but the existence of these democratic, instead of feudal, roots were a fertile soil for the Norwegian labor movement to build on. Kokkvold (1968*) sees the historical task of the labor movement in Norway as a continuation of this democratic trend under the changing conditions created by the arrival of industrialization at the end of the previous century.

Norway's industrial development started relatively late. In the 1850's some small textile factories and machine shops existed which did not expand because their market was restricted to a limited home market. The topography of the country and the scattered population made transportation too expensive. In addition the lack of iron ore and coal explains why heavy industry did not develop in Norway's industrialization process. This shortage was the basic reason that no large industrial enterprises working on the basis of labor-saving methods of production were created at the end of the nineteenth century. A marked change in the industrial structure of Norway only

1. The study resulting in this book was made under a fellowship from the U.S. Social Science Research Council with supplementary support of the David Dubinsky Foundation. However, the conclusions, opinions and other statements in this dissertation are those of the author and are not necessarily those of the funding institutions.

occurred during the last years of the first decade of this century. It was the development of cheap hydro-electric power for industrial use which enabled the economy to 'take-off' and establish modern type of industry and attract foreign capital for industrial use. In the period between 1900 and 1915 the number of industrial workers increased from 84,658 to 136,941 (Lafferty, 1971, 38). Until this time no industrial infra-structure existed because of the reliance on primary industry like fishing and forestry. In 1910 the primary industries plus shipping still contributed 31.6% to the gross national product. The next three tables give some impression of Norway's industrial development in this century.

Table 1. Labor force sectors as percentage of total labor force.*

	Primary sector	Industrial sector	Service sector
1870	56	16	28
1890	49	22	29
1900	41	26	33
1910	39	25	36
1920	37	26	37
1930	36	26	38

(Lafferty, 1971, 43).

Table 2. Percentage of employment by major branches.*

	1930	1938	1950	1970
Primary industries	42.6	38.8	30.3	14.8
Manufacturing and mining	17.1	18.8	24.–	25.8
Building and construction	4.8	5.9	7.5	13.0
Merchant navy	3.1	3.1	3.2	3.9
Services, governmental and private	31.7	32.7	34.1	42.5

(Thorsrud, 1972, 6).

* Lafferty and Thorsrud do not define their categories in exactly the same manner. (Thorsrud, 1972, 6).

Table 3. Percentage of contribution to gross national product.

	1910	1930	1939	1950	1970
Agriculture, forestry, fishing	24.7	17.7	12.4	15.4	6.3
Manufacturing, mining	22.9	24.3	26.6	30.9	25.5
Commerce	14.9	13.–	14.9	13.1	16.9
Merchant navy – transport	6.9	10.8	13.5	12.4	10.6
Governmental and private service	13.9	14.1	13.6	13.7	23.4

The relatively late but stable industrial growth in Norway did not lead to class conflicts and the distressed economic conditions for industrial workers as in most other industrialized contries. The transition from the primary sector to the industrial sector was rather gradual and this gradualism prevented mass unemployment of unskilled labor and its concentration in urban industrial slums. From the late 1800's a strong relationship existed between the trade unions and the Norwegian Labor Party (DNA).[2] This close co-operation between the trade union and the political labor bodies is a characteristic feature of the Norwegian industrial relations system. The formal liaison between the Federation of Trade Unions (LO) and DNA is a committee of cooperation discussing all important trade union and political questions. DNA with a social democratic platform stayed in government continuously from 1935 to 1963, except during the five years of German occupation in the second World War. This close link with the political party in power and the early recognition of trade unions by the employers provided the basis for a stable political and industrial relations system.

The Norwegian population was 3,972,944 at the beginning of 1974. This small population and the low population density, 12 people per km², are fundamental background characteristics of Norway. Half of this population is concentrated in the south eastern area around the capital of Oslo. The Norwegian capital is the biggest city with 600,000 inhabitants. The labor force in December 1973 was 1,680,000 (Statistisk Sentralbyra) and Kassalow (1974) estimates that about 65% of this labor force belongs to a trade union.

The Norwegian Federation of Trade Unions (LO) was founded in 1899. The typographical union, like in many other countries, is the oldest Norwegian union and was founded in 1872. Today the number of national unions

2. For a useful history of the Norwegian trade union movement see Bull (1956).

affiliated to LO is 40. Total LO membership in the middle of 1974 was just
a little under 620,000. Membership figures for the five largest LO member
unions are:

Iron and metal workers	98,552
Municipal employees	96,493
Building industry workers	47,189
Commercial and office employees	42,949
Chemical industry workers	37,348

(Fri Fagbewegelse, 1974*, 14, 15).

These five unions account for over 50% of the total LO membership. Companies are organized following industrial principles with as result that
within the individual enterprise one, or sometimes two unions represent all
the workers. In the case of two unions present, each union caters to a clearly
identified constituency, for example white collar versus blue collar workers.
LO is indisputably the most powerful authority in the Norwegian union
structure. This powerful position is the result of a very high degree of centralization in the trade union movement which is evidenced e.g. by the fact
that LO has the right to approve strikes. Strikes which have not been approved do not receive financial support from the federation.

A strong national organization is particularly urgent for the many small
Norwegian unions which are unable to run effective secretariats themselves.
Membership in the national federation provides them with effective administration in a wide range of areas. The 1973 LO Congress adopted a
recommendation regarding reorganization of the trade union structure with
a view to reducing – by 1985 – the present number of affiliated unions from
40 to 7. These unions would cover the manufacturing industries; building,
construction, agriculture and forestry; sea and land transport; commerce
and tourism; public employees; civil servants; and culture and education.

For the individual worker the local union branch naturally is the most
visible part of this highly centralized national trade union structure. The
activities and influence of union locals differ from company to company. In
the larger undertakings, e.g. in the metal and chemical industries, the local
union activities are well developed and the shop steward committees play
dominant roles in plant level industrial relations and collective bargaining.
The local and district agreements in Norway serve the function of applying
the formulas agreed upon at the national and industry levels to the local

situation. Local agreements go into great detail regarding wages, wage classification systems, working hours, overtime and numerous other allowances. The agreements do not however put limitations on management prerogative in the deployment of labor. Management decisions regarding work assignment seem to be much more free from constraint than in the U.S. Local shop stewards (tillitsman, literally meaning 'trust man') seem to have considerable influence despite the fact that not many specific rights are provided for in the contracts. At the plant level like the national level, the influence of the shop steward is considerably enhanced by informal cooperative processes. The unions in Norway are well represented on the shop floor in the larger undertakings and their power exceeds considerably the rights which are contractually given to them. Management in Norway seems generally in favor of strong local unions and the shop stewards are seen as the representatives of all employees.

The Norwegian employers are organized in a strong national federation NAF (Norwegian Employers' Federation). In 1972 53 employers' branch organizations were members of NAF. These branch organizations are organized roughly along the same lines as the national unions within LO. A small number of big companies like Norsk Hydro, the big chemical concern which is vastly expanding in the oil field, are directly affiliated to the NAF. The branch organizations have about 8500 companies as member which together employed 367,000 persons in 1972 (NAF, kalender, 1973*). NAF only represents the employers' interests in labor related areas. The employers' broader economic and financial interests are represented by another strong national organization the Norwegian Industry Federation (NIF).

The Basic Agreement (Hovedavtale), sometimes called the Norwegian constitution of industrial relations, regulates the basic arrangements between the employer organizations represented by NAF and the trade unions united in LO. The Basic Agreement in addition to its regulations reflects an attitude of tolerance on both parties. The first agreement of 1935 was an important step in a development towards a degree of accommodation between LO and NAF, which is so characteristic for the Scandinavian industrial relations systems. This first agreement paved the way for a permanent and institutional relationship between the two national federations. The agreement contains provisions of a substantive as well as a procedural character. After the 1966 major revisions the agreement consists now of three parts. The first part covers provisions concerning the right to organize and the duty to bargain collectively. It includes a peace obligation during the life of the collective agreements and it regulates the election and position of the shop stewards vis a vis management. Furthermore, there are provisions governing the position of new members of the NAF and LO, voting procedures on draft collective agreements, questions of employment, the check-off, sympathetic strikes etc. Paragraph 9 of the 1974 agreement contains the most central stipulation regarding 'cooperation'[3] between members of the two organizations at the local level:

'To the individual person it is of the greatest importance that the feeling of unity between him and the undertaking is strong and alive, and this is also a prerequisite to effective production. In order to obtain such a feeling of unity it is important to have practical ways of discussing common problems and of mutual information in matters of interest to the management and to those working there. Through this cooperation, the employees, through their experience and insight, should take part in increasing efficiency, reducing production cost, improving the competitive capacity of the firm *and create a more satisfying place to work and a work organization which is both efficient and meets the human need for development.*'[4]
(Hovedavtale, 1974*, 15).

The second part of the Basic Agreement, added in 1966 and called the 'Cooperation Agreement', provides guidelines which operationalize the intentions of the above excerpts from Paragraph 9. The role, functions, and membership of the work council within each company is regulated in detail. Also the functions of a national Cooperation Council which consists of 3 representatives each from LO and NAF are specified in this section. The Cooperation Council is an informative and consultative body for the cooperation-institutions, mainly work councils, at the level of the undertaking. The Cooperation Council:

'shall assist in making the individual work councils function in the best possible way. It shall encourage educational measures which will promote cooperation and also put at the disposal of the cooperation agencies of the individual undertakings experiences of others and research results which may be of practical importance to them. Representatives of research and science may be assigned to the Council by the parties'.
(Hovedavtale, 1974*, 46).

This Cooperation Council is jointly financed by the LO and NAF.

The third and last section of the Basic Agreement contains joint provisions on procedures for solving disputes on the interpretation and duration of the

3. Cooperation is a key word in Norwegian industrial relations. Cooperation between management and union definitely does not imply company unionism. It suggests that both parties maintain their complete organizational independence but work together to solve problems of mutual interest.
4. Emphasis added. Author's translation.

agreement. The agreement extends for four years. Traditionally LO termi-
nates the agreement by a written notice six months ahead of the expiration
date to set the stage for renegotiation. The Basic Agreement between LO and
NAF forms the first part of all wage agreements between either the central
organizations themselves or between their member organizations. The first
section of the agreement is only valid for organized workers while the regulations in the second part regarding cooperation within the individual enterprises holds for both organized and unorganized workers. In practice however this distinction does not seem to lead to any differences in treatment
between organized and unorganized workers. The high percentage of workers
organized (80% within the average manufacturing company) is clearly responsible for this.

In the 1973 Basic Agreement negotiations LO demanded union shop arrangements for firms where 50% or more of the employees were union members. After strong NAF opposition this demand was watered down to a fee
to be paid by non-union members. This too was rejected by the employers,
but they agreed not to oppose the principle of introducing a trade union fee
by legislation (LO News Bulletin, December, 1973, 81). Passing of such
legislation is highly unlikely however, given the current power balance in
parliament between the 'left' and 'right' parties. The agreed upon 1974 Basic
Agreement provides for the strengthening of the position of workers' safety
representatives, who will be entitled to stop production if a situation occurs
endangering life and health of workers at the shop floor. The Basic Agreement also includes new provisions supporting the principles of job redesign
as experimented with in the Cooperation Project. Other provisions strengthened the security of shop stewards and workers' representatives on the different representative organs.[5]

Both NAF and LO are very active in the organization of educational programs for their members. To provide a broader financial basis for these
efforts NAF and LO agreed in 1970 to establish the Information and Development fund. The objective of the fund is to 'implement and support measures for the promotion of information and training in Norwegian working
life'. The financing of the fund again reflects the 'cooperative' spirit. Every
employee, whether organized or not, has Kr. 0.50 per week deducted from
his wages: in addition the employer pays Kr. 1.00 per week for every employee in his undertaking. This arrangement secures that every week Kr. 1.50
($ 0.30) per employee is invested in education. Similar arrangements have
also been made for the public sector so the yearly amount reserved for educa-

5. The next chapter discusses these changes in more detail.

Table 4. Strike statistics 1958-1974.

Year	Number of strikes and lockouts*	Workers involved	Man-days lost
1958	16 (5)	12,541	57,798
1959	18 (9)	2,113	47,616
1960	12 (9)	656	2,417
1961	19 (6)	22,910	423,082
1962	8 (−)	1,069	81,121
1963	8 (−)	10,588	226,394
1964	3 (−)	230	1,310
1965	7 (2)	591	8,927
1966	7 (4)	1,392	5,207
1967	7 (3)	436	4,720
1968	6 (1)	486	13,514
1969	4 (3)	824	21,636
1970	15 (10)	3,133	47,204
1971	10 (8)	2,519	9,105
1972	9 (2)	1,105	12,315
1973	11 (0)	2,380	11,400
1974	6 (1)	15,000**	310,000**

(Source: NAF).

* In brackets the number of strikes that were 'illegal' given collective agreement stipulations.

** This figure for 1974 is provisional.

tion in this manner exceeded Kr. 30,000,000 ($ 6,000,000) in 1972. The distribution of the money is supervised by a committee of six members, three from LO and three from NAF. A small part of the fund goes to mutual educational undertakings like some programs to promote cooperation within the individual establishments. The remaining money is divided equally between LO and NAF. Joint courses are currently being provided in the following areas: labor-management cooperation at the enterprise level, preparatory courses for members of the corporate assembly and the supervisory board, and courses in job design which focus at the practical aspects of some of the findings of the Cooperation Project. In this course companies send a 'vertical slice' (Emery and Emery, 1974) for participation. A typical company delegation to this week long seminar generally consists of one or two workers, the local shop steward, a supervisor, the personnel manager or production engineer, and a representative of top management.

The Norwegian industrial relations system[6] has been one of the most peaceful in Europe since the second World War (Fisher, 1973). The number of strikes and man-days lost have been rather low as is indicated in table 4. Many possible reasons, in addition to the lack of a feudal tradition and the social and cultural homogeneity of the Norwegian population, can be listed for Norway's peaceful industrial climate. Six broad categories are particularly important:

1. size of the country
2. industry characteristics
3. nature of the economy
4. legislative framework
5. existence of a legal alternative to bargaining
6. social democratic reform ideology

The small size of Norway and its economy lead to the situation where almost any strike of some size is looked upon by the general public and the government as a threat to the nation's economic stability. In larger countries a strike must be of a considerably larger size and longer duration before it is perceived by the government as a threat to the nation's welfare. A small size economy is directly affected by a strike of any size. This leads to a psychological climate which facilitates quick intervention by government, in particular through mediators, in cases where the parties do not reach agreement themselves.

The relative small size of the majority of Norwegian companies and the lack of heavy industries like steel, mining, car manufacturing etc. very likely contribute to peaceful industrial relations. Small size companies, of all Norwegian companies only 90 firms in industry employ over 500 workers, traditionally have more peaceful labor management relations, partly because

6. Following Dunlop (1958, 383) an industrial relations system 'is comprised of three groups of actors – workers and their organization, managers and their organizations, and governmental agencies concerned with the work place and work community. These groups interact within a specified environment comprised of three interrelated contexts. The technology, the market or budgetary constraints and the power relations in the larger community and the derived status of the actors. An industrial relations system creates an ideology or a commonly shared body of ideas and beliefs regarding the interaction and roles of the actors which helps bind the system together.'

Table 5. Distribution of companies in industry and mining by number of employees (1972).

Number of employees	Number of companies
< 5	5489
5–9	3135
10–19	2169
20–49	1803
50–99	773
100–199	401
> 200	293

(Statistisk Sentralbyra).

Table 6. Unemployment statistics.

Year	Average number unemployed	Percent of labor force
1960	17,097	1.2
1961	13,048	0.9
1962	15,184	1.1
1963	17,725	1.3
1964	15,540	1.1
1965	13,358	0.9
1966	11,933	0.8
1967	11,419	0.8
1968	16,462	1.1
1969	15,605	1.1
1970	12,458	0.8
1971	12,193	0.8
1972	14,812	1.0
1973	12,811	0.8

(Statistisk Sentralbyra).

of simpler communication structures and a higher degree of direct management-worker interaction.

The stable Norwegian economy with almost continuous full employment in the last 30 years clearly provides a fertile soil for peaceful industrial relations. Table 6 presents the employment picture over the last thirteen years.

Unemployment levels for 1974 and 1975 are estimated well below those of the previous years. In August 1974 only 0.6% of the total labor force was unemployed. In contrast to the 8750 persons registered as unemployed the number of vacancies reported to the public labor exchange offices was 10,350, which was 18% higher than at the same time last year (LO News Bulletin, September 1974). This stringent labor market is caused by a low growth of the labor force. The expected rapid economic expansion due to the huge oil deposits located in the Norwegian sections of the North Sea will contribute to continuing labor shortages. The Norwegian government has been able so far to keep the number of foreign workers at less than 1.3% of the labor force. In 1973 there were 21,200 foreign workers; only 8000 of them were from other Scandinavian countries. LO's official position is against increasing the number of foreign workers from non-Scandinavian countries[7] and supports instead a number of measures to improve the living conditions for those foreign workers who have already established themselves in Norway. Related to the huge oil finds in the North Sea there is a growing activity in construction of drilling and production platforms primarily engaging ship- yards and construction firms. Large investments have been made in the development of a petro-chemical industry which is scheduled to start pro- duction in 1977-1978. The Norwegian government, strongly supported by DNA and LO, plans to keep the rate of future oil exploration and exploita- tion down to a pace which the economy can absorb without serious dis- ruptive effects on the present employment and income structures. No in- crease in immigration is assumed. To what extent a higher labor force parti- cipation of women can offset the increased demand for labor in this super right labor market, is an unanswerable question at this moment. Develop- ments in the fall of 1974 however seem to indicate a need for a larger influx of foreign labor to Norway (Aftenposten, September 18, 1974*).

Social legislation in a large number of non-wage areas (unemployment benefits, social security, vacations etc.) considerably reduces the number of issues to be covered in the collective bargaining agreements. In addition to the well developed body of social legislation the Labor Dispute Act which originated in 1915, revised in 1927, and supplemented by many revisions over time, has proved to be a surprisingly impartial law without any long- term favoritism. This in sharp contrast to Anglo-Saxon legislation, the U.S. labor legislation is an example, which is developed by the passing of legisla- tion either 'to suppress the rights of one side or to support the claim of one

7. Nordic labor market agreements assure a free movement of labor between Sweden, Norway, Iceland, Finland, and Denmark.

or the other party' (Dorfman, 1966, 101).[8] All labor legislation in Norway is drafted in committees which include representatives of the workers' and employers' side. If bargaining breaks down the Labor Dispute Act provides first for mediation. In case the latter is unsuccessful the law stipulates either voluntary arbitration or the passing of a special act by parliament for solving the interest dispute by compulsory arbitration. The Labor Dispute Act also governs the operation of the Labor Court. Only rights disputes, in contrast to disputes concerning interests, can be brought before this Labor Court whose decisions are binding. The Court consists of seven judges; three neutral ordinarily qualified judges, two appointed by LO and two by NAF. The case load of the Labor Court is minimal.

When 'labor' has a majority in Parliament the potential threat of going the alternative route could make management's position in the bargaining process a little more flexible. NAF clearly prefers collective bargaining over the use of legislation (Selvig, 1972*). More control over the bargaining process is probably one of the main reasons for this attitude. The existence of the alternative route makes it not always necessary for the unions to get the 'extreme' out of the bargaining process. The passage of the 1972 co-determination legislation is a clear case in point. In contrast to negotiations for the Basic Agreement and regular collective bargaining, there is no agreement necessary with the employers if the labor movement decides to gain new rights through the legislative process. The close relationship with DNA made it possible to solve on the political level numerous important social problems for which it otherwise would be difficult to find solutions without having resort to sweeping labor conflicts. The political route is also an important 'face saving' device for both LO and NAF. Legislation basically defends LO against its own left and NAF does not have to cope with the criticisms of its conservative members. In contrast to bargaining agreements the two federations do not have any direct political responsibilities for legislation.

Finally the social democratic reform ideology opens up the possibility for cooperation between management and labor. Naturally this 'cooperation spirit' is both a cause and effect of the other mentioned categories. A foreign observer can only be impressed by this spirit which is not only reflected in

8. The Labor-Management and Disclosure Act of 1959 (Landrum-Griffin) signalled a new era in U.S. labor legislation. The U.S. public policy orientation shifted 'from a pressure group response toward the assertion of a more autonomous interest, neutral as between the claims of business and unions' (Barbash, 1970, 1134). This new orientation is often described as positive public policy.

the Basic Agreement, but more importantly manifest itself in the many daily contacts between members of NAF and LO. These contacts take place in the cooperation committees, in many parliamentary committees, and in numerous advisory boards to important social institutions like schools, hospitals etc. In addition to these formal arrangements many problems are solved during informal 'get togethers' between the representatives of the two organizations. That this integration sometimes leads to a lack of clarity for 'rank and filers' and foreign observers alike is not surprising.

As Table 4 (p. 8) indicates strike activity in 1974 was considerably higher than in any of the foregoing years. The number of strikes did not increase but the duration and number of workers involved resulted in a considerable increase in the total number of man-days lost. Three conflicts were responsible for almost 80% of the number of man-days lost in 1974. Long strikes by electricians and workers in the meat processing industry and a short conflict at Norsk Hydro involving more than 5000 workers were responsible for the major part of the number of man-days lost. A number of developments can be listed which have contributed to this unusually high number of man-days lost in 1974. The high inflation rate combined with 'low' real wage increases in the past few years led to a strong motivation to improve real wages. The return to industrywide bargaining without a national framework agreement provided the stronger unions with additional powers at the bargaining table. The positive economic outlook for Norway in the next decade, mainly caused by the huge oil deposits located in the North Sea and the strong expansion of a number of oil related industries contributed to the unions' demands for an increased share of the new wealth. The return to industry bargaining weakened LO's ability, which it had so successfully used in the post-war years, to 'control' its member unions. This controlling or disciplining function of LO under a system of a national framework agreement is another factor explaining the peaceful industrial relations record in Norway.

Finally harder bargaining and more industrial action can be expected because of SV's (Left Wing Socialist Front) presence at some shop floors, in particular in the metal industry. The presence of these groups outside the 'labor movement' forces some national unions, and also the LO to take a harder stand in negotiations, this in addition to the 'unrest' created in the traditional system by these new groups themselves.

The social democratic labor movements in the Scandinavian countries seem to have lost some of their traditional grip on society. In Norway the position of DNA and LO in favor of joining the EEC was of crucial importance for the further desintegration of their social democratic electoral

base. Norway had earlier applied for EEC membership in 1962 and 1967
when in 1970 the Norwegian Parliament (Storting) endorsed a proposal by
a coalition government to join the EEC by an overwhelming majority of 132
to 17 votes. It became soon evident that this vote did not adequately represent the balance of opinion in the country. The farmers feared increased
competition in a weak agricultural sector while the strong fishing interests
feared that Norway might lose its dominant position in an industry where
the Norwegian resources are the richest in Europe. The proposed signing of
the Treaty of Rome was seen by many as a loss of Norwegian sovereignty.
Despite this public sentiment all LO and DNA leaders were staunch sup-
porters of joining the EEC. Inside these two organizations resistance developed which joined forces with the New Left. This group agitated against a
surrender to 'monopoly capitalism' and campaigned under slogans like
'Norway is not for sale'. The general resentment was directed against Norway becoming a heavily industrialized country with the concomittant problems of pollution and the power of big enterprises. On September 23-24,
1972 a referendum was held on the issue. About 80% of the electorate record-
ed its vote, which revealed a majority of 53.5% against entering an enlarged
EEC. Oslo and the three surrounding counties supported joining, however
all other counties rejected the proposal, in some rural areas with majorities
of over 70%. This result represented a strong defeat for the Norwegian social

Table 7. Results of the 1973 parliamentary elections.

Party	Votes	Percentage	Diff. −73/−69	Seats	Diff. −73/−69
Labour (DNA)	759,848	35.3	−11.2	62	−12
Conservatives	375,782	17.5	− 2.1	29	0
Centre Party	237,073	11.0	0.5	21	1
Christian P.P.	261,869	12.2	2.8	20	6
Liberals	76,155	3.5	− 5.9	2	−11
New Liberals	73,855	3.4	3.4	1	1
ALP (Anti Tax Payers)	107,747	5.0	5.0	4	4
Left Wing Socialist Front (SV)	241,816	11.2	6.7	16	16
Red Election Alliance	9,360	0.4	0.4	0	0
Others	10,004	0.5	0.4	0	0

(LO News Bulletin, September/October, 1973).

democratic block and in the meantime united Norway's political left wing in opposition to DNA. For the 1973 Parliamentary elections the left wing parties, including the Communists, the Socialist People's Party, and the so-called Information Group against EEC that had withdrawn from DNA, united themselves in the Left Wing Socialist Front (SV) and surprisingly pulled over 11% of the popular vote.

Until this election DNA had received in the post second World War elections an average of 45% of the total popular vote. The 35.3% represented a post war low for the DNA. A recent Gallup poll (Spring 1974) indicates a further decline of DNA support which was then estimated around 30%. These electoral indicators reflect the problematic position of DNA and the labor movement as a whole in the early 1970's. The social democratic platforms do not seem to be adapted to the new set of complex problems in a modern industrial society. Several observers (e.g. Aftenposten, September 9, 1974*) underwrite a drastic need for political renewal within Scandinavian labor movements. The attainment of some degree of affluence for the average Norwegian and the declining proportion of the labor force in the manufacturing sector has somewhat eroded the traditional basis for the Norwegian labor movement. The success of the Anti Tax Payers in the 1973 election represents an increasingly wide-spread concern with the current tax burdens. Rising income levels have lead to a situation where skilled workers are also being confronted with the progressive taxation system. The new parties on both the right and left side of the political spectrum seem to indicate an erosion of the traditional class solidarity which determined to a large extent the success of the Norwegian labor movement. This class solidarity is apparently being replaced by a loyalty to a number of narrower interest groups.

One of the organizational issues confronting DNA and LO is the continuation of the collective membership arrangements. Under this arrangement workers of certain union locals are automatically a member of DNA unless they sign an affidavit that they do not want to be a DNA member. Only 15% of the total LO membership (620,000) is a member of DNA through this arrangement. However in the important Oslo area collective membership accounts for about 80% of the DNA membership. The unions have therefore full control over the party committees in the Oslo area (Arbeiderbladet, December 10, 1973*). Pressures exist both within the trade union movement and the Labor Party to end this particular arrangement. This collective affiliation of union locals with DNA is strongly resisted by the more individualistic oriented white collar groups. The issue of collective membership belongs to the broader question whether or not an union should be a political organization. The increasing number of white collar employees within LO provides a strong force in favor of breaking up some of the traditional ties between LO and DNA, and support changing the union federation into a non-political organization. Similar arguments are heard within DNA where some believe that the general appeal of the party is reduced through its strong connections with the trade unions. If LO and DNA choose to increase their services for the growing group of the higher paid and mostly white collar workers the emerging Left Wing Socialist Front (SV) will almost certainly gain support in some of the traditional strongholds of the labor movement like the metal unions. If on the other hand the choice is made to maintain the links with these traditional bases, a cleavage with the white collar groups would result. The situation in Norway is more complicated than in Sweden where a strong non-political union (TCO) caters to the white collar employees. In short the discussions within LO and DNA are mounting around two issues:

A. Is the labor movement going to cater specifically to the white collar groups?
B. If 'A' is answered positive what organizational changes have to take place in LO and DNA to cater to this new group?

Underlying this whole discussion is the question of how real is the cleavage between the white and blue collar groups in modern Norway? It cannot be expected that the Norwegian labor movement will make clear choices in the near future. The practical policies will continue to focus at some unidentified middle group, thereby increasing the political viability of SV. The labor movement's leadership currently seems to perceive the danger of potential losses to the 'right' (e.g. Anti Tax Payers) greater than possible losses to the 'left' (SV). The increase in size of the white collar unions within LO will probably contribute to the start of a depoliticizing process within this organization. How DNA will react to the above trends is impossible to predict at this moment. Strong internal divisions are apparent as the party is searching for a successor to its chairman for a decade, Bratelli (prime minister till 1976). The strong degree of integration between DNA and LO is highlighted again by the fact that the president of LO, Aspengren, was one of the three members of the DNA's searching committee for a new party leader.

This changing environment also contributed to the important LO decision in 1973 to have, for the first time since 1961, separately negotiated industry agreements, instead of the centrally coordinated negotiations. The latter used to set all wage rates of any national importance. This decision meant the end of a Norwegian solidaristic wage policy. The stronger unions had pressed for a return to individual agreements. Naturally the weaker unions, among them the clothing workers, resisted the end of the solidaristic policy. The unions in the low wage industries were the prime beneficiaries of this policy. Not surprisingly NAF reacted in a reserved manner to the return to industry bargaining without a national framework. It could possibly be argued that the beneficiaries of a solidaristic policy are the lower paid workers on one hand and the employers in the high wage sector on the other. This despite the fact that wage drift has been an important feature of the previous 'low wage profile' settlements.

In the early 1950's Galenson (1952, 339) characterized the Norwegian labor movement as a mere administrative organ of the state. Indeed in the immediate post-war period the three actors in the Norwegian industrial relations system, government, trade unions, and employers, cooperated to a significant extent in the rebuilding of the war damaged economy. This degree of cooperation and integration should not be exaggerated however. Galenson's qualification is more than outdated today. The social democratic philosophy still determines the major goals of the Norwegian labor movement. This social democratic philosophy with gradualism as its key aspect certainly facilitated trade unions and employers, particularly at the central levels, to work out a 'modus vivendi' which consists of cooperation in areas where there is perceived common interest and confrontation on those issues where the interests are clearly opposed, like in wage bargaining. The unusual wave of strikes in 1974 underlines the antagonistic-militant attitude with regard to economic issues. The Norwegian trade union federation has been able to combine an integrative-institutional with an antagonistic-militant attitude in its approach to labor-management relations at the national level. This combination of attitudes requires a fairly equal balance of power between the two national federations representing employers and workers respectively. LO's strong relationship with DNA is a critical factor in this power balance which facilitates cooperation on issues of an integrative nature. 'Wage bargaining' in Norway is relatively less complicated than in the U.S. as many issues are provided for by legislation (unemployment and sickness benefits, pensions, vacations and holidays etc.). Taking these issues out of the bargaining process possibly introduces more space for cooperative issues in labor-management relations. LO leaders apparently have been successful in wearing the integrative-institutional and antagonistic-militant 'hats' at the appropriate time.

The effectiveness of this approach is being challenged by the Left in both the trade unions and political parties. These critics disagree with the effectiveness of the established LO and DNA leadership in furthering the workers' interests.

Cooperation requires a balance of power. To what extent this power balance exists at the local level is difficult to assess. The power of the local unions in Norway is easily underestimated because of the lack of 'rights' at the plant level. Especially in the larger plants the local shop stewards have built a strong informal position which provides for enough of a power base to engage in successful cooperation. Also the very thigt labor market contributes considerably to the power of the union local. In the numerous smaller companies a wide diversity of labor-management relations exists. Here we find authoritarian ruled factories, examples of benevolent paternalism, and situations where unions are strongly represented at the shop floor. If no adequate power balance exists cooperation at the local level can easily result in the union losing its institutional independence.

Compared to other national industrial relations systems Norway is characterized by a high degree of cooperation and integration, especially at the central level, between employers, trade unions and government. This cooperation should not be exaggerated however. Different attitudes are prevalent on issues where there is no perceived commonality of interests.

2. The start of the cooperation project and other postwar developments in industrial democracy in Norway

OVERVIEW
Production council and its predecessor – the industrial democracy debate around 1960 – the start of the Cooperation Project – Emery and Thorsrud's evaluation of board representation – the Aspengren committee – the 1966 Basic Agreement – the corporate assembly – conclusions.

As a precursor to the developments after the Second World War the Norwegian Parliament passed a law in 1920 which established work councils in industrial companies. In these work councils management and labor were supposed to cooperate on productivity problems in the best interests of the factory and its employees. The work council idea was received with little enthusiasm by the employers and with great suspicion by the trade unions, which found collective bargaining a more effective manner of furthering the interests of their members. Despite the fact that more than 100 such councils were established and that the law remained on the books until 1963 these work councils never achieved any real importance in Norwegian industrial relations (Larsen and Hansen, 1972).

The Second World War and its aftermath created conditions which were favorable for the development of a cooperative spirit between management and labor. The joint exile of top employer representatives and union leaders during the war, the cooperation in the resistance movement, and the enormous task of rebuilding the Norwegian economy after 1945 were strong forces bringing the two parties closer together. Despite this cooperative spirit NAF and LO reacted rather skeptically to the proposals by the Gerhardsen labor government in 1945 to establish joint production councils based upon the British and U.S. examples during the war. Only the threat by the Gerhardsen government to pass legislation to create such councils brought LO and NAF together and a Production Council agreement was signed in 1945. Initially all companies with more than 25 employees were required to have a production council. This limit was extended upwards in later years, first to 50 employees and later to 100. The goal of the production council was 'to work towards the most efficient production and reduce unnecessary waste of materials, manpower, and machines' (Landsradet, 1954*, 3).

The attitudes of both LO and NAF towards the production council can best be described as 'Janus face'. NAF on one hand supported the production council idea, but on the other hand resisted implementation because LO and DNA in their respective congresses in 1946 stressed the council as a tool to raise the consciousness of the workers. LO also showed two faces. Outside the official government and LO-NAF meetings it often gaven the impression of an increasing hostile attitude toward the employers. This radical stance was caused by a then rather strong and vocal Communist minority within the labor unions. At the local level employers boycotted the councils because they feared that most issues to be discussed in the councils would go well beyond practical production policies (Stenersen, 1972*). In the early 1950's the more radical utterances of LO and DNA started to disappear.

Approximately 800 production committees were established. Using some rather crude averages the following evaluation can be given: These 800 committees were about 1/3 of the potential number, of these 800 about 1/3 worked very well, 1/3 had very sporadic meeting schedules, while the remaining 1/3 were totally inactive (Ryste, 1973*(b), and Larsen and Hansen, 1972). Studies evaluating the operation of the production councils cite apathy among employees and employers as the basic reasons for the disappointing performance of most councils. Publications by the National Committee for Production Councils indicate that this LO-NAF committee perceived the functions of the production council as a kind of 'idea-box' to further a company's productivity (e.g. Landsradet, 1954*). Local union representatives were not a member of the production council. This lack of union representation clearly explains why local union support for these councils was limited. In 1948 the National Committee stated explicitly that production councils should not be perceived as a step towards increased workers' control (Ryste, 1973*(b)). Ryste (1973*(b)) and Stenersen (1972) conclude that with a few exceptions production councils were mostly inactive. Where active, they were generally ineffective in improving labor – management relations at the plant level.

In the late fifties and early sixties a wide debate about industrial democracy developed in Norway.[1] This debate ultimately resulted in: The start of the Cooperation Project in 1962; changes in the 1966 Basic Agreement LO-NAF introducing a work council with broader goals than the production council but still with rather limited powers; and the passing of legislation in 1972 providing for representation on the board of directors for the workers and

---

1. Chapter I of Emery and Thorsrud (1969) gives a good illustration of this debate in Norway through numerous quotes from politicians, employers, and trade unionists.

creating a corporate assembly in industrial companies with more than 200 employees.

Under pressure from DNA and LO the labor government appointed in 1956 the so-called 'Frihagen Committee'. The mandate of this committee was to evaluate whether or not the Company Law should be amended in order to provide for worker representation on the board of directors. NAF mounted a strong campaign against worker representation on the board with as result that the Committee did not produce any proposals at all. Instead NAF made some concessions in the Basic Agreement negotiations which resulted in a new arrangement that meetings of the local shop steward committee and the board of directors are held once a year or as often as one of the parties expresses a wish for it. NAF's position was, and still is, that industrial democracy can only be attained through cooperation between labor and management and not through the enforcement of externally imposed legislation.

Around 1960 a complex political and economic situation developed in Norway. In the labor movement the radical wing was overruled completely on the issue of nationalization of private industry. Alienation had become a topical issue in industrial democracy discussions, but there was no consensus about which policies to follow in order to increase industrial democracy. In national politics DNA's position was weakening so that the continuous reign of the Labor Government ended in 1963. The trade unions realized that this political situation minimized the chances of legislating industrial democracy. NAF was becoming aware that despite its concessions in the Basic Agreement negotiations the labor movement continued to discuss other avenues towards industrial democracy. Economically Norway started to feel the influence of the EEC. Market conditions for firms within metal manufacturing, textile industries, and pulp and paper looked particularly unfavorable (Thorsrud, 1970). Increasing concern at the national level was voiced regarding the status of Norwegian industry. The lack of natural resources and the increased international competition necessitated basic changes in industry.

These were the environmental conditions when Thorsrud introduced his ideas about job redesign and industrial democracy. Decentralization and the creation of more autonomous jobs would not only reduce alienation and start a democratizing process, but also release the human resources of the better educated work force and increase productivity. Thorsrud's intervention[2] was timely and the strength of his proposals was that all parties in-

2. Thorsrud's dynamic and somewhat charismatic personality clearly contributed to the acceptance of his proposals by LO and NAF. In addition the fact that he had the 'Right'

volved in the national industrial democracy debate could identify with at least some of the elements in them. Industrial leaders in general evaluated positively the references to the release of human resources and the possible favorable impact of job redesign on productivity. NAF supported the ideas rather strongly because shop floor democracy was perceived as a preferable alternative to board representation or at least could delay the labor movement's efforts to introduce such representation. The LO leadership possibly was least enthusiastic, but the fact that there was no consensus in the labor movement on how to achieve industrial democracy and the specific references to alienation and shop floor democracy, led to a weak endorsement of Thorsrud's ideas by LO. The Technical University of Trondheim provided a forum where union leaders and representatives of industry were exposed to Thorsrud's thinking. These developments led in 1962 to the establishment of a LO/NAF joint committee. Its first major task was to draft a research program on industrial democracy which would be executed by the Trondheim Institute for Industrial Social Research lead by Thorsrud. Later the research was transferred to the AFI (Work Research Institutes) in Oslo where Thorsrud became research director. Initially this research program, named the Co-operation Project, was jointly financed by LO and NAF. In later years government contributed half of the total cost and in 1967 the state became fully responsible for the financing of the project. Local experiments are of course the responsibility of the individual company but government pays the salaries of the researchers at the AFI, thereby eliminating the traditional loyalty conflicts of management consultants. Thorsrud (1970) gives great weight to the relatively simple centralized influence-structure in Norway which not only facilitated the spreading of his ideas but made also possible the later social experimentation at the plant level and the innovative role the researchers could play through these unusual social and financial arrangements.

Under pressure from the union representatives the LO/NAF joint committee decided that first an investigation should be launched to deal with formal representation arrangements in management. This phase of the research project was labeled Phase A. Phase B should deal with the conditions for personal participation at the immediate shop floor level. This latter phase would only start after completion of Phase A. In Phase A of the project,

---

credentials for LO, being a member of DNA and an activist in the resistance movement in WW II, facilitated the unions' federation's formal endorsement. It is maintained by some that the union leadership at that time did not thoroughly understand Thorsrud's proposals in all their ramifications but that they went along with them because of his credibility.

which is reported in Emery and Thorsrud (1969)[3] representation of workers on the boards of companies was evaluated. A number of state-owned Norwegian companies where workers did have board representation since 1948 was studied and the findings were supplemented by research reported in the literature about worker representation on the board of directors in other countries, in particular Germany. The conclusions of Phase A were very pessimistic and clearly in line with Thorsrud's notions with respect of the importance of the immediate job content in any democratizing process.[4] Thorsrud and Emery, the latter a member of the Tavistock Institute, chose as their main evaluation criterion: the impact of board representation on the shop floor workers. It was not surprising that this impact was found to be negligible. Emery and Thorsrud (1969) also documented the difficulties and role conflicts which confront the worker representatives on the board.

The emphasis on the conditions for personal participation at the shop floor level was deliberately choosen. Thorsrud and his collaborators believed that individual activation and learning at the job were necessary conditions for a well functioning system of board representation. It was a tactical decision to start the democratization process at the bottom of the organization instead of at the top. This emphasis however led to a relative neglect of functions of formal representation systems other than the activation of shop floor workers. Emery and Thorsrud (1969) briefly mentioned union and social class representation of the worker interest, the latter through the Labor Party, but in their subsequent research no attempts for a broader evaluation of these representative systems and their relationship to shop floor participation were undertaken.

The findings of Phase A[5] set the stage for the industrial experimentation at the shop floor level which undoubtedly was the main research task of the Cooperation Project. Emery and Thorsruds' (1969, 1) view that 'social science is as yet (not) particularly well equipped to deal with problems of board representation' reflects however a not very well documented judgement in favor of job redesign.

In 1964 Phase B was started. The joint LO/NAF committee agreed to start experiments in job rediesgn in a number of selected companies. The participation of the workers involved in these experiments was voluntary. Another

3. This book was originally published in Norwegian in 1964.
4. This does not imply any critique on the integrity of the researchers involved. It only serves to underline the fact that so often in social science the choice of a certain conceptual model builds in an 'a priori' bias with respect to the range of ultimate conclusions.
5. In an inteview Thorsrud emphasized that the conclusions of this study must be seen in the Norwegian political context of 1963.

primary principle was that both management and the workers could terminate an experiment if either of them wanted to do so.

At the same time that the Cooperation Project Phase A was started, discussions within the labor movement about industrial democracy continued. The national union of iron and metal workers clearly took the lead in the discussions within the trade unions. In 1961 LO and DNA established a joint committee, the 'Aspengren committee', which presented in 1962 an elaborate discussion document on industrial democracy to all local party organizations and branch unions. Table 8 presents the preference as stated by the local party and union branch organizations.

The expressed preference for the extension of the Basic Agreement was based upon the opinion of the local organizations that this would strengthen the position of the shop steward and the local union organization. The response to the first alternative was influenced by the fact that many thought the proposal, as phrased in the discussion document, in conflict with the Norwegian Constitution. After having received this feedback on the discussion document from the local organizations the Aspengren committee submitted in 1963 its preliminary report, stating that further action for industrial democracy should take place along three parallel lines:

'1. Training in order to enable the employees to make better use of their right of participation.
2. The extension of the existing arrangement for consultation in accordance with the Basic Agreement between LO and NAF.
3. Changing the organizational structure of firms through legislation. In the opinion of the Committee the most important element would be to create a new body – the corporate assembly – to be a forum where employees could meet the capital owners for discussions and decisions.'
(Aspengren, 1973, 3).

These conclusions are interesting because they reflect the essential characteristics of the policies of the Norwegian labor movement and the relative unimportant role the Cooperation Project has played in the industrial democracy debate within this movement. First, the Aspengren committee favored both the extension of the Basic Agreement and legislation as means to achieve industrial democracy. It looked for cooperation with NAF through the Basic Agreement, but also realized that in order to challenge the managerial prerogative and the existing social order, more than labor-management cooperation was required. These questions 'must be solved by legislation' (Halverson, 1971, 2). Second, the labor movement did not consider nationalization any longer as an effective avenue toward industrial democracy. Nationa-

Table 8. Preferred avenues to industrial democracy by local organizations.[6]

	Preferences	
Alternative as provided in discussion document	DNA chapters (55)	Union locals (147)
1. Legislation to create a corporate assembly	9	49
2. Extension of the basic agreement	23	51
3. Extension of the power of the production council	7	15
4. Combinations of the above or no preference	16	32

lization and public interest representation on the board was advocated in a large number of pamphlets and a couple of books by Anker Ording (1965) which were rather influential in trade union circles. Neither of these suggestions were included in the committee's conclusions. Nationalization was considered ineffective and also not feasible politically; public interest representation was excluded because it was judged in conflict with certain stipulations in the Norwegian Constitution. Third, the Aspengren committee's conclusions and the debates that followed did not pay any attention to the outcomes of Phase A and the shop floor democracy ideas underlying Phase B of the Cooperation Project LO/NAF. The Cooperation Project, with the possible exception of the Phase A report on board representation in the early sixties, has never reached any degree of prominence within the Norwegian labor movement. NAF has been using the findings of Phase A as an argument against board representation (see e.g. NAF, 1965*). NAF also integrated rather successfully the job design ideas in a number of job design seminars. Throughout the sixties and early seventies the labor movement spent most of its energies in the struggle for a corporate assembly and board representation.

In 1965 the joint LO-DNA committee (the Aspengren Committee) submitted its final report which, in addition to the above mentioned three parallel lines of action, included an outline of suggested amendments to the Company Act which would increase workers' participation. The committee proposed the establishment of a corporate assembly in all undertakings irrespective of

6. This table is compiled from information presented in a 1963 report by the LO-DNA joint committee entitled *Uttalelser fra LO og DNA grunnorganisasjoner*.

their being under public or private management and irrespective of their
judicial character. The Aspengren committee explained its final recommendations as follows:

'The organization of undertakings today is based on the principle that capital alone shall
influence the governing bodies of the company. It is the opinion of the committee that this
form of company organization is obsolete and it does not conform with our modern con-
ception of democracy and the importance of labour. The committee will propose that for
the organization of undertakings the joint-stock company in the first place – be changed
through legislation, in order that the employees also inside the company will obtain a
forum where they will participate together with the capital owners in the discussions and
decisions on matters concerning the company.
    The committee does not believe that such a reform alone will create industrial demo-
cracy. It is even necessary to warn against expecting too much at short term of such a
reform of the organization of companies. Nevertheless, it is the opinion of the committee
that such a reform will be an important part among others of the development of democracy in our industry.
    The committee will propose that a democratic corporate assembly shall replace the
present committee of shareholders' representatives in joint-stock companies.
    The corporate assembly should be something different from, and more than a passive
control body. Its importance should be underlined by the fact that the corporate assembly
alone should elect the Board of Directors and it should be the body to which the Board
should be answerable.'

(Aspengren, 1973, 4).

The essence of the corporate assembly idea was to change the shareholders'
representation, which in Norway was organized in the form of an optional
committee of shareholders' representatives, from being a controlling institution for the shareholders to a forum for cooperation, where the employees
in the business enterprises are on an equal footing with the shareholders. In
the spring of 1965 the Aspengren committee's recommendations were endorsed in the discussions of the LO and DNA Congresses.
    In 1966 the Basic Agreement LO/NAF was revised and a new section on
cooperation was added. The main aspects of this new cooperation section
were the replacement of the production council by a work council and the
establishment at the national level of a Cooperation Council LO/NAF with
as major goal 'to provide information and advice for cooperation organizations (work councils) in the factories and to ensure that the work councils
function satisfactorily' (LO, 1971, 24). The introduction of a Cooperation
section in the Basic Agreement reflects a change in emphasis at the national
level from the postwar prominence of productivity to cooperation as a goal
in itself. Work councils must be established in undertakings employing more
than 100 employees. In undertakings with 100-400 employees management
may appoint up to 5 representatives. The employees also have 5 representa-

tives. The chairman of the shop steward committee is an ex-officio member of the council. The chairman of the council must be elected by the members. The main difference between the work council and the preceding productivity council is the broadening of its advisory and informative functions in areas not directly related to productivity (annual reports, expansion plans etc.) and the integration of the local union into the work of the council. It is explicitly agreed upon that the work council shall not deal with questions of wages and working hours or disputes on the interpretation of collective or work agreements. In large companies department councils can be established in addition to the central work council. This is extremely important in order to provide more workers an opportunity to participate in matters related to their direct work setting. Section 32 of the Basic Agreement defines the activities of the work and department council as follows:

'The works council is an advisory and informative body. The main task shall be through cooperation to work for the most efficient production possible and for the well-being of everybody working in the undertaking.
    With this object in mind, the council, among other things, deals with:
a. Informative and confidential reports from the management on the financial status of the undertaking and its standing within its branch of industry, as well as other matters of importance for production and sales possibilities. In this connection, written financial statements are given to the same extent as they are normally given to the stockholders through the financial account at the annual general meeting. If the members of the council request it, they shall be entitled to return to the account at a later meeting of the council.
b. Questions in connection with the activities of the undertaking, major changes in production plans and methods, questions of quality, the development of products and plans for expansions and restrictions or reorganization which are of major importance to the employees and their working conditions . . . The council shall work for sound and correct rationalization. Through informative work it shall promote understanding for the social and industrial importance of this.
c. Suggestions and measures for improving employee safety and health, also suggestions for improving the protective and health promoting measures within the framework of the Workers' Protection Act . . .
d. Social measures (welfare).
e. Questions regarding vocational training for the employees including information to new employees.'

(LO-NAF, 1974*, 42-43).

According to the Basic Agreement a work council must meet at least once every month. Research directed by the Cooperation Council in 1968 involving 381 companies showed that on the question 'How often does the work council meet?' 161 companies did not give an answer, while from the remaining 220: 51% had six meetings or less a year, 49% had seven meetings or more a year. A general consensus exists that the work councils operate a

little more effectively than the production councils but Ryste (1973* (b), 6)
warns: 'Of course much can be said about the employers' will to give information and discuss issues openly in the work council, but there is also the
question whether the employees themselves have been active enough in using
the opportunities created by the Basic Agreement'.

The national Cooperation Council established by the 1966 Basic Agreement has six members, three appointed by LO and three by the NAF. The
Council has its own full time secretariat which consists of three persons. The
activities of the councils cover the providing of information, training, and
coordinating research in order to stimulate cooperation at the plant level.
In 1968 the Cooperation Council became also responsible for the spreading
of the results of the Cooperation Project LO/NAF.[7]

At the end of the sixties and early seventies the public debate about industrial democracy again became very prominent in the media and in political
parties. Industrial democracy had become such an important political issue
that the platforms of all Norwegian political parties included proposals to
end the contrasts between the rights of citizens in the political democracy and
the position of employees in the industrial undertakings. In many of these
discussions the proposals by the Aspengren Committee (see p. 24) to create
a new democratic body within undertakings (the corporate assembly) played a central role. DNA and LO launched a national campagin in 1971 under
the motto 'Democracy in Everyday Life'. In the spring of the same year the
findings of the Eckhoff committee were made public. The Eckhoff committee
was a tripartite body of seven members which was appointed in early 1968
by a non-socialist Norwegian government to study and report on the issue
of industrial democracy. The Supreme Court Justice Eckhoff was chairman
of this committee which included trade union representatives Aspengren and
Hansen. The three neutral members on the committee together with the employers' representatives did not recommend any radical changes in the Company Act in order to give workers the right of codetermination. The union
representatives dissented and proposed, following the Aspengren committee
recommendations, the introduction of legislation providing for the election
of a democratic corporate assembly and workers' representation on the undertakings' board of directors. In the fall of 1971 the labor minority government took up the views expressed by the dissenting trade union members of

7. To avoid confusion with regard to the numerous cooperation institutions: the Cooperation Project was started in 1962 as result of a separate agreement between LO/NAF. The
Cooperation Council was established by the 1966 Basic Agreement and is basically a service
organization to local work councils.

the Eckhoff committee and turned them into a legislative proposal. It was however not clear at that time where the necessary votes would come from to achieve passage of the bill. To the considerable surprise of many Norwegian observers, the Center Party not only agreed to support the bill, but proposed amendments to expand its scope. These amendments provided for employee representation on the board as well as on the corporate assembly. The LO had rejected the idea of minority representation on the board as the entire solution, but did not object to such representation as an addition to the creation of corporate assemblies. The amended bill was passed and the revised Company Act became effective January 1, 1973.

The main aspects of the amendments to the Norwegian Company Act will be briefly outlined below. The new provisions give employees in companies with between 50 and 200 employees a right of electing at least two representatives to the board of directors. In companies with more than 200 employees a corporate assembly shall be established. This corporate assembly shall have at least 12 members of which 2/3 will be elected by the general meeting of shareholders and 1/3 by and among the employees of the company. The corporate assembly is an executive organ with decision making authority in matters concerning investments which are substantial compared with the company's resources. It is also the firm's final authority on decisions involving rationalization or alteration of the operations as will entail a major change or reallocation of the labor force. On all other matters the corporate assembly can make recommendations to the board of directors. The corporate assembly shall also elect the board of directors and if 1/3 of the members of the assembly so wish, this election shall be on a proportional basis. This means in practice that the employees have secured through these amendments 1/3 representation on the board of directors. Neither the general meeting of stockholders nor the board of directors has the right to overrule the special type of decisions which are taken according to the new provisions by the corporate assembly.

These new regulations apply only to approximately 250 joint stock companies within mining and manufacturing industries which together employ more than 150,000 persons. Modified forms of this legislation will over time be introduced to cover both public and private enterprises in all areas of economic activity. As of Fall 1974, no evaluation can yet be made about the operation of the corporate assembly. A majority of the 250 companies (circa 70%) have introduced an assembly in their organizational structure. Neither LO nor NAF officials see the new law as likely to change the Norwegian industrial relations scene. Capital owners still have a majority voice in both

the corporate assembly and on the board of directors. Despite its antagonistic attitude towards the legislation NAF is currently rather active in stimulating its members to take a constructive attitude towards the corporate assembly (Skard, 1973*). NAF fears that an inactive management attitude
towards the corporate assembly might hasten the introduction of new legislation in this area. Both LO and NAF have launched ambitious education and
training programs in order to prepare their members for their new functions
in the corporate assembly.

This overview of postwar developments in industrial democracy in Norway hopefully reflects the great value Norwegians attach to the democratic
ideas. In most policy statements by NAF, LO, the government, and the
political parties, 'workers' participation, industrial democracy and similar
concepts are used to cover something taken for granted as a value in itself,
and not so much as a specific plan or instrument to achieve other objectives
and values' (Thorsrud, 1972, 21). The attempts of the Norwegian labor movement to democratize industry are however definitely characterized by a lack
of overall strategy and no declaration is available from either LO or DNA of
what they ultimately hope to achieve. The corporate assembly legislation
was the product of a labor movement which engages more in opportunistic
tactics than in building a well-developed strategy to achieve full industrial
democracy. The labor movement has been unwilling to specify the form of
society and the type of production organization it stands for. DNA needs
political slogans for its electoral campaigns which can be supported by LO.
Industrial democracy has fulfilled this slogan function fairly well, without
giving it a somewhat precise content. The leaders of the Norwegian labor
movement still deplore the 'inherent' contradictions of the capitalist system
at the ideological level, but their policies reflect a pragmatism which approaches the dominant outlook of U.S. unions. The labor movement thereby
possibly becomes an important bulwark for the preservation of, a more
humane, private enterprise system. The Norwegian labor movement has become a countervailing power to private ownership interests. The political
debates and developments in the area of industrial democracy indicate that
the labor movement does not want to supersede this countervailing position
by defining a clear alternative for the current organizational structures in a
highly industrialized country. LO President Aspengren reflected recently the
Norwegian labor movement's difficulties in specifying long-term goals: 'We
are willing in principle to take up the debate again about what is socialism?
This dispute is an old bone of contention within labor movements of all
countries, one which certainly has not strengthened these labor movements.'

(Fri Fagbewegelse, 1975*, 3). This unresolved debate makes the development of a long-term strategy to further industrial democracy extremely difficult. Future proposals in this area can therefore not be expected to go beyond isolated tactics to increase the workers' influence without seriously challenging the current methods and organization of industrial production.

In the past two decades the Norwegian labor movement, given the political constraints, has been rather successful in implementing its separate proposals to increase democracy in industry. In the last ten years ambitious training and education courses for workers have been set up, the Basic Agreement LO/NAF was revised to create a work council on which the shop stewards are represented, and the 1972 amendments to the Company Act operationalized the proposals for a corporate assembly. To evaluate the impact of these changes is extremely difficult. Wide differences exist in the operation of local work councils and corporate assemblies. However, all changes together have opened up a wider range of options for workers and their unions to participate and possibly influence important organizational decisions, if they have the desire and abilities to do so.

Thorsrud's intervention in the political debate and the subsequent start of the Cooperation Project in a sense depoliticized the industrial democracy notion by stressing the integrative nature of his concrete job redesign proposals. The Cooperation Project nicely conformed to the social democratic reform ideology of the Norwegian labor movement. It was based upon the following general premises: the parliamentary model *by itself* is unable to bring industrial democracy into the firm; there are clear issues of cooperation between labor and management, but conflict will certainly not wither away in the near future; solutions therefore must be sought within a mixed but basically privately owned economy (Lange, 1969*). Despite this fit with the social democratic reform ideology the Cooperation Project never reached a prominent status within the trade union movement. The start of the Cooperation Project was a clear reaction against a national political situation, but the political debate continued and LO and DNA accepted the corporate assembly proposals as a major political goal. NAF which generally had a more favorable posture towards the Cooperation Project was forced through these political developments to spend much of its resources to counter the labor movement's proposals. In addition both organizations were naturally taken up by their usual day-to-day business. LO and even more so the national unions remained ambivalent towards the job design ideas and under pressure from LO the Cooperation Council added in 1972 the following statement to a brochure describing some of the ideas behind the Cooperation Project: 'For LO and NAF it is not a question whether the experiments with autonomous groups should be continued, but how fast can we justifiable proceed' (Samarbeidsradet, 1972*, 19). In 1972 LO still tried to control the diffusion process, most likely because of the difficulties to fit it in with their normal policies. Recent elaborate statements by LO President Aspengren on industrial democracy (Aspengren, 1973 and 1974) do not even refer to the Cooperation Project ideas as an element in the LO efforts to further industrial democracy. When asked, LO leaders seem to be very positive in their attitudes toward job redesign, however they have been unable to make the issue a lively one within their own organizations.

The Norwegian experiences indicate again that good intentions and agreements at a national level are by themselves not sufficient conditions to start job design experiments at the local plant level. Diffusion of the ideas did take place in Norwegian industry in the early 1970's despite LO attempts in the Cooperation Council to control the diffusion. Political factors play the dominant role at the national level, but economic considerations determine whether or not an individual company will start with job redesign. The Cooperation Project has been useful in giving national coverage to Thorsrud's ideas and the first four experimental companies demonstrated to management and local unions that cooperation in this area can have advantages for both parties. Whether or not to start a job redesign process remains however a local management decision mainly based upon economic criteria, this in spite of the national agreement LO/NAF on the Cooperation Project.

Finally it should be mentioned that the issues raised by Thorsrud in the early sixties preceeded the discussions on alienation, shop floor democracy, humanization of work, and the quality of working life in most other countries by almost a decade.[8] The next chapter will focus in detail at the specific contributions of Thorsrud and his collaborators at the AFI to this field.

---

8. In the U.S. for instance this debate started in 1972 with the Senate Hearings on Worker Alienation, the International Conference on the Quality of Working Life at Arden House, New York, and the controversial HEW report Work in America (HEW, 1973) as its main instigators.

3. The job design ideas behind the cooperation project

OVERVIEW
The major AFI design notions – the indebtedness to the Tavistock Institute – other job design approaches – evaluation of the AFI approach from a theoretical point of view – strength and weaknesses of AFI approach – values in job design and conclusions.

The job design ideas upon which the Cooperation Projects are based have an eclectic nature. Neither a general theory of organizations nor a well defined theory of job design can be identified in the work of the researchers at the AFI. What can be distilled however are a number of principles which the 15 or so researchers of the AFI apply in their work with organizations and the people within them.[1] Therefore in order to evaluate and criticize these principles, I first have to present and summarize them in some kind of framework. In reading this chapter, it should be remembered that what is being evaluated are not *the* AFI principles of job design, but a personal interpretation of the core principles distilled from writings, publications, presentations, and interviews with several researchers at the AFI. In my analysis heavy weight is given to the work of Einar Thorsrud, the initiator of the projects. Of course Thorsrud's thinking has developed since the early sixties and what is presented below is hopefully representative of the current 'state of the art', including many of the ideas upon which the early experiments were based. This chapter restricts itself to an analysis of the theoretical aspects of the job design approach developed at the Tavistock Institute and put into practice by the AFI researchers. Results of the application will be treated in later chapters.

The approach to job design of the AFI is founded on the well known assumption (see e.g. H.E.W., 1973) that many of todays jobs are unnecessarily fragmented, specialized, and hierarchically controlled. Fragmentation, specialization, and hierarchical control lead to a lack of freedom and autonomy for the individual worker, who is not able to develop his full human, but also productive, potential under these conditions. Jobs of this type are considered

1. There is no agreement among these researchers about 'the best way' of approaching job design, however there exists certainly some consensus about the principles as presented below.

incongruous with the demands of the modern well educated labor force and incompatible with environmental pressures for flexible organizational structures.

The goal of job redesign in the context of the Norwegian Cooperation Projects is formulated as: 'that of improving the conditions for personal participation in the work situation with the aim of releasing human resources' (Thorsrud, 1970, 67). It was expected that this could be attained by eliminating or reducing some of the Tayloristic design elements in industrial jobs. Based upon an extensive review of the psychological literature and earlier work of the Tavistock Institute (Rice, 1958; Trist et al., 1963) Emery and Thorsrud developed a number of psychological job requirements which are used in the evaluation of individual jobs. A job is 'better' when more of these requirements are met. The following requirements were developed:

'1. the need for the content of a job to be reasonably demanding or challenging in terms other than sheer endurance, and to provide a minimum of variety (not necessarily novelty);
2. the need for being able to learn on the job and to go on learning;
3. the need for some minimal area of decision-making that the individual can call his own;
4. the need for some minimal degree of social support and recognition in the work place;
5. the need for the individual to be able to relate what he does and what he produces to his social life; and
6. the need to feel that the job leads to some sort of desirable future.'

(see e.g. Emery and Thorsrud, 1969, 105).

These requirements are used as criteria for evaluation of individual jobs. They 'represent a minimal set of criteria according to which we could design and evaluate jobs in concrete technological settings' (Thorsrud, 1973, 8). The requirements play an important role in the process of job redesign because they are used both as indicators of where the jobs under analysis are deficient, and as a set of evaluation criteria measuring the success of the redesign. It is assumed that by meeting these requirements to a larger extent the individual worker will be better motivated and take initiative where necessary. Meeting the six requirements will therefore also improve the total organizational functioning.

The 'open socio-technical system' approach is the analytical tool used in studying existing job designs in order to locate those areas where changes can be introduced which will meet the job requirements to a greater extent. Both the 'socio-technical' and the 'open system' notions can be traced to earlier work done at the Tavistock Institute.

Several studies carried out by members of this institute showed clearly that the introduction of technical change without due regard to the social implications resulted in a failure to realize the expected improvements in organizational performance (Trist and Bamforth, 1951). In the study by Trist and Bamforth and also in the work by Rice (1958) the interdependence between the technical organization of work and the social patterns of the work force was clearly shown. In both studies the introduction of new technology was unsuccessful because there was no 'fit' between the technical and social subsystems. Also in both cases groups were introduced which had the responsibility for a number of tasks. The classical paradigm of industrial job design 'one man – one job' was broken up by the assignment of a number of tasks to a group of workers. In the case of the coal mine (Trist and Bamforth) this was exactly the organizational structure that existed before the introduction of the new technology. In these studies the simultaneous analysis of both the technical and social aspects of tasks led to the introduction of work groups. Work groups 'fitted' the particular technology and contributed to improved performance of the organizational unit. The basic principle which emerged from these studies was that a one-sided optimization of the technical system will result in less than optimum performance because of the neglect of the social system. Joint optimization of the two systems will lead to more optimum performance.

The 'open system'[2] aspect of the approach reflects the conceptualization by Emery and Trist (1965) of the enterprise and the work group as units which are in constant interaction with a larger environment. The role of management (at the enterprise level) and supervisor (at the level of the work group) is primarily concerned with relating their unit to its environment through the regulation of exchanges at the unit's boundary. This external regulation is the primary task of the supervisor so that the members of the work group become more fully responsible for the internal regulation. In more practical terms a supervisor should spend most of his time working with the larger organization, instead of engaging in close supervision of how tasks are executed.

The 'open system' notion directs the researcher to study both the interdependencies between the work group and the larger organization, and also the interdependencies between the members of the work group itself. The matrix of variances (Engelstad, 1970* and 1972) is a useful tool for the analysis of key interdependencies and to find out where these variances can

2. The system concept is rather ill-defined in the work of the AFI researchers. The concept is used as an 'educational device' (Thorsrud in interview) to underline the numerous interdependencies within organizations and between organizations and their environment.

be controlled within the organization. Major elements of an 'open socio-technical system' analysis of a department have been the:

- 'variations in inputs and outputs of departments;
- estimates of relative importance of different variations;
- establishing the primary tasks of departments;
- description of work roles, status, recruitment, and training;
- analysis of communication networks;
- analysis of attitudes to work;
- analysis of the system of remuneration, wages, bonuses etc.'
(Thorsrud, 1973, 12).

The autonomous work group concept clearly has a central place in the Co-operation Project. Of course there is always a certain amount of dependence between the autonomous work group and the larger organization. Practically, the autonomous group can only be autonomous with respect to its own direct job setting. Thorsrud and Emery (1970*, 222-224) underline that in order to be able to talk about autonomy it is vital that limiting conditions are given in the form of product specifications and other 'agreements' as regards supplies to and from the group, and that the resources the group manages are fixed. Based upon earlier work by Gulowsen (Gulowsen, 1971*) four main criteria of group autonomy are distinguished. The group can decide:

1. which working methods will be used;
2. who shall belong to the group (the personnel selection);
3. who shall take charge of directive duties if they come into prominence (leadership);
4. who shall perform which duties (internal task allocation).

In addition Thorsrud and Emery (1970*) specify three general conditions which have to be fulfilled if the autonomous group is going to exist:

1. the group must adequately comply with the above listed four criteria of autonomy.
2. the group must be able to meet the demands of the larger organization for in and outgoing supplies. The group must also be able to take care of the duties normally carried out by a supervisor.
3. group actions must operate in such a way that they stipulate sufficient agreement, solidarity, and stability within the group.

Gulowsen (1971*, 1972) studied a number of existing autonomous groups and concluded that autonomy is a one dimensional property of work groups. Gulowsen's ten criteria for autonomy formed a Guttman scale implying that certain basic criteria for autonomy have to be fulfilled first, in order to reach higher degrees of autonomy. Group decisions regarding individual production methods, internal leadership, recruitment, and internal distribution of tasks were found to be prerequisites for higher degrees of autonomy in the decision making areas of group production methods, starting time, additional work loads, external leadership, and quantitative and qualitative goals (Gulowsen, 1972, 387). In the last couple of years the autonomous group notion does not seem to play such a dominent role as in the first decade of research. Limited success in application under different technologies is the major cause. Over time the term autonomous work group was realistically expanded into partly autonomous work group and later altered into partly self-governing work group.

The key concepts in the AFI approach towards job design can now be summarized as follows: A simultaneous analysis of both the technological and social systems, the emphasis on interdependencies between the different work tasks and between the work group and the larger organization, the stress on a work group with a number of tasks as the essential building block of an organization. In particular the concentration at the relationship between a work group and its tasks instead of focusing at the one-man-one-job relationship distinguishes this approach from earlier job design theories. This focus on the group brings more organizational variables under control which can be changed in the process of redesigning jobs. The outerlimit of job redesign is clearly extended by focussing at the group level intead of the individual level. Herbst (1974b) labels this increased room for maneuvering 'free space'.

In their application of the Tavistock notions Thorsrud, Emery, and colleagues at the AFI expanded the original notions in three important directions: First, the traditional role of the management consultant was altered into the role of a collaborative researcher. This change in role was facilitated through the independent financial position of the researchers. Initially the projects were financed by L.O. and N.A.F., but after two years the state guaranteed the income for the researchers of the AFI. It is questionable if traditional consultants would have been able to obtain the confidence of management, unions, and workers involved. Second, the redesign process was opened up to all the parties involved. In particular participation of the workers whose jobs are the target of redesign and their local union representatives, is one of the pre-conditions for an experiment. In some instances the researchers withdrew their support if they felt there was no adequate participation of the workers and local union, and the experiment had come under full control of management. Third, the evaluation criteria for the measurement of success of job redesign were expanded. The success of redesign is measured, among others, in terms of the psychological job requirements (see p. 34) and not in the first place by traditional productivity measures.[3]

What are some of the practical changes in job design resulting from the application of the above described theoretical approach? The practice of socio-technical analysis is probably more flexible than outlined earlier. In any event an attempt is made to locate those elements in the work design which are relatively easy to modify in order to increase the level of autonomy in the individual jobs. In the first step of this change process alterations will be made close to the individual job. In later stages the work group, department, and larger organization become the focus of analysis in that these levels put many constraints on the organization of the individual job. In order to further change job content, these levels, because of the many interdependencies, have to be included in the change process. In addition to, and sometimes part of, the attempts to introduce work groups with some degree of autonomy, the following concrete reorganizations have been implemented in an attempt to make work better in terms of the psychological job requirements:

A. *Technical decisions being delegated*
   1. planning of processing methods;
   2. ordering of materials;
   3. work scheduling and task allocation;
   4. inspection and quality control;
   5. setting up of machines;
   6. machine maintenance;
   7. cleaning of work area.

B. *Decisions regarding personnel and work conditions being delegated*
   1. hiring of new employees;
   2. disciplining of group members;
   3. planning of shift composition;
   4. start of work hours;

3. This does not imply that the other parties involved in the experiments use the same criteria as the researchers. I will return to this in the next chapter.

5. authorizing time-off and decisions regarding vacations;
6. selecting of supervisor or teamleader;
7. eliminating 'busy work' through more autonomy.

In particular the delegation of technical tasks and the increase of tasks which can be executed by each worker requires that group members become multi-skilled. Multi-skilling is a very central element in many of the experiments. Multi-skilled workers improve flexibility within the work group which allows workers to make more decisions, but also is a form of upgrading and enhances promotion chances. Better skilled and higher qualified labor does not require very close supervision. In order to increase the number of decisions the workers can make it is necessary sometimes to eliminate the position of the supervisor or chargehand or change his role in a manner which requires him to focus most of his attention to the relationships between the work group and the larger organization instead of closely supervising subordinates. Multi-skilling obviously facilitates job rotation, and the delegation of some decision making power to lower organizational levels clearly has much in common with changes suggested in the job enrichment literature.

As described in the previous chapter Thorsrud connected these notions of job design to shop floor democracy and thereby to the national industrial democracy debate in the early 1960's. Industrial democracy according to his views should be introduced at the shop floor level and generate a broader process of organizational change which would make organizations more democratic. Job redesign utilizing the above mentioned principles was seen as a first step in a continuous process of social change. Increased freedom and autonomy at the shop floor were seen as a pre-condition for the start of further democratizing processes inside organizations. Job design was put in the context of organizational and even societal change processes. This in sharp contrast with other leading approaches towards job design which will be described next.

In a somewhat dated (1955) but still useful survey study Davis, Canter and Hoffman (1972) attempted to find out which job design criteria were most often used in industry. The content of individual tasks was generally specified:

1. 'So as to achieve specialization of skills.
2. So as to minimize skill requirements.
3. So as to minimize learning time or operator training time.
4. So as to equalize and permit assignment of a full work load.

5. In a manner which provides operator satisfaction (No specific criteria for job satisfaction were found in use).
6. As dictated by considerations of layout of equipment or facilities'.
(Davis, Canter and Hoffman, 1972, 71-72).

Tasks generally were combined into specific jobs using the following guidelines:

1. "Assign each employee a specific operation as a full-time job.
2. Assign each employee a specific group of elements of an operation as a full-time job.
3. Assign each employee one particular element of an operation as a full-time job'.
(Davis, Canter and Hoffman, 1972, 72).

Limiting the content of the individual's job was one of the guiding principles
for most companies. The emphasis on the minimization of skill requirements,
education, learning time, and the stress on a narrowly defined task clearly
indicates that the work of Frederick Taylor and his scientific management
approach were in 1955, and very likely still are today, the dominating job
design principles in industry. Taylor (1923) focused at the 'one-man-one-job'
relationship and recommended specialization, including a clear separation
between thinking and doing, and reduction of the level of analysis to mere
physical movements. Like the pattern of machine work, human motion was
broken into elements, and movements of arms and legs were ordered into
'one best way' of usage. The 'scientific' logic was that the work of each man
could be measured by itself, an impersonal 'standard time' could be established and pay could be computed without bargaining on the basis of the
amount of work done and the time taken to do it. Work at the shop floor
was reduced to doing. The planning, organizing, leading, and controlling
functions were separated from the work process and placed inside the management hierarchy.

A strong reaction against scientific management came from a rather heterogeneous group of academics, consultants, and managers whose combined
efforts are commonly referred to as the 'human relations movement'. Building upon some of the findings of the research at the well known Hawthorne
Western Electric factory (Roethlisberger and Dickson, 1939) this group rejected Taylor's 'logic of efficiency' and substituted it by a 'logic of human
sentiment', which would as well considerably increase productivity. The social
and communal needs of the worker were the central focus here. Managers
were advised to create a community feeling in their factories, show personal
interest in their workers, and harness informal group processes to achieve

higher productivity. Despite the fact the 'human relations movement' maintained itself into the early sixties it has had only very limited impact on the design of individual industrial jobs. Human relations should be credited however for bringing the human equation back into organizational thinking.

The following school in this historical order is often labeled 'participative management'. McGregor (1960) and Likert (1961) were the main proponents of this school which focused almost exclusively at the supervisor-subordinate relationship. An employee-centered supervisory style in which supervisor's focused their attention on the human aspects of their subordinates' problems and on building effective work groups, was found to be superior over the traditional job centered leadership style. A participative leadership style involves sharing more information with subordinates, eliciting their ideas, encouraging interchange among them, employing general rather than close supervision. The essential task of management was, through this employee centeredness, to arrange things so people at work could achieve their own goals by accomplishing those of the organization. Likert and in particular McGregor went not much beyond leadership and the result was that the technological factors and the time and motion studies remained dominant in designing the individual's job.

The work of Herzberg (Herzberg, Mausner, and Snyderman, 1959) can be credited with focusing for the first time at the individual worker and his immediate job. Building upon Maslow's hierarchy of needs, in particular upon the self-actualization notion, Herzberg reported that the content of the individual job determines to a large extent worker motivation. This line of psychological thought and the work of Argyris (e.g. 1959) gradually developed into a body of job enrichment, job enlargement literature.[4] This literature proposes changes in structure of the job in order to increase the level of responsibility for the individual worker. Variety, challenge, wholeness of task, and feedback are reintroduced into the tasks in order to improve organizational performance and job satisfaction. At about the same time the Tavistock Institute and Louis Davis in the U.S.A. were developing their 'open socio-technical system' approach which so strongly influenced the researchers at the AFI in Norway.

What has been the major contributions to the field of job design by the Norwegian researchers and their predecessors at the Tavistock Institute?

Theoretically the technical and social systems are perceived as equally

---

4. See for a good summary Hackman and Lawler (1971).

changeable in nature. Technology[5] is not merely treated as a given in the design of a job. Both technical and social changes can be necessary in order to attain a better 'fit' between the social and technical systems. The awareness that technology can be changed is a conceptual breakthrough in the field of job design. Taylorism adapted the worker to technology, human relations and participative management comfortably neglected technology, and job enrichment lead to changes in job content within a given technology. The socio-technical approach has the potential to achieve structural changes which go well beyond changes in leadership style and traditional delegation of authority. The socio-technical approach can also be perceived as an attempt to integrate social psychological theories of organizations and structural sociological theories. The former (e.g. Likert, McGregor and Argyris) focuses primarily at the individual and group levels of the organization thereby neglecting macro organizational variables like size, technology,[6] control system, and the impact of the environment. The socio-technical approach is successful in integrating some aspects of both theories. Its thrust is at the group level, but it does not study the group in a vacuum. The importance of the autonomous work group can be regarded as building upon the Hawthorne studies which so clearly identified the importance of the informal group and its impact on social norms. The Tavistock approach tries to harness some of these group processes by reducing organizational prescription and giving the group autonomy in some areas of direct production and personnel. The change process focuses at the technology, the task structure,

5. Technology generally means here the machinery, the physical hardware with its standardizing and controlling impact on the behavior of the individual workers. This usage of the term technology is more restricted than its general use in the sociological literature. Following Blauner (1964, 6) technology signifies 'primarily the machine system, the level and type of mechanization, but it includes also the technical know-how and mechanical skills involved in production'. Using these criteria Blauner distinguishes between craft, machine, assembly-line, and continuous process technologies. Clark's (1972, 36) definition of technology includes only 'the raw materials to be transformed, the equipment, and the buildings within which the production processes take place'. Perrow's (1967) definition of technology has the most general applicability. Perrow (1967, 195) means with technology 'the actions that an individual performs upon an object, with or without the aid of tools or mechanical devices, in order to make some change in that object'. Perrow discerns two aspects of technology which vary independently: the number of exceptions that must be handled, and the degree to which search is an analyzable or unanalyzable procedure.

Because of the applied nature of the Norwegian job design projects technology is used here in its least abstract meaning: the machines and physical equipment on the shop floor. For more theoretical purposes Perrow's definition is to be recommended. His definition makes technology an operational concept also far those organizations where machines do not dominate the work organization (e.g. hospitals and civil service agencies).

6. Technology used here in a more Perrowian sense (see note 5).

the work group, and the potentials of the individual worker. The emphasis on the work group and the treatment of technology as changeable has considerably increased the room for maneuvering in the job design process. In addition the incorporation of the link between the work group and the larger organization opens up new possibilities to improve the 'fit' between the social and technical systems.

The addition of the psychological job requirements to the established technical and economic criteria introduced a new, long neglected, dimension to the criteria used in the evaluation of job design.

The open-endedness of the socio-technical system approach increases the general applicability of this approach in a wide number of different work settings. The AFI approach differs substantially from other job design theories in that it does not prescribe one particular structure as a solution to all problems in this area. The 'open socio-technical system' approach is an important tool of analysis. Instead of providing clear cut solutions, it gives insights into the organizational interdependencies and in many aspects is more a process of designing jobs than a method which provides ready made solutions. In socio-technical changes 'the starting off point is initially only partly known and what is aimed at can not from the start be completely specified, imitation of a ready made solution may not only be inappropriate but may also inhibit the diffusion process' (Herbst, 1974b, 13). This flexibility clearly adds to the general applicability of the approach.

Thorsrud et al. opened up the job design process to the workers immediately involved and also gave the local trade union some control over it. This is a major contribution in the implementation of the Tavistock notions. The context of the Cooperation Projects made this participation of course a necessity from an institutional point of view. In many instances an official vote among employees was taken whether or not to start a project within a company or department. In all cases local action groups, including shop steward and worker representatives, were responsible for the development of the change process. The institutional framework for redesign includes a national agreement between L.O. and N.A.F., and separate agreements on the local level stating that the workers themselves shall have the opportunity to participate in the planning and evaluation of new systems. The introduction of participation and some degree of control over the design process in an area where technical expertise has played such a dominant role, is an easily underestimated contribution of the Cooperation Projects. Herbst (1970, Ch. II, 8) describes the role of engineering under this new approach as being 'no longer concerned with complete detailed specification but with minimal critical specification'.

After this evaluation of the contribution by Thorsrud and his Norwegian collaborators I will now turn to the theoretical weaknesses inherent in this approach to job design.

The 'open system' notion emphasizes system performance. The idea of 'best fit' between technology and social organization is based on the assumption that optimal system performance and the 'right' technical organization coincide with those job conditions under which the social and psychological needs of the worker are satisfied. System performance is the critical variable. Under some circumstances improving the social and psychological aspects of a job, particularly when they are badly neglected, could lead to better performance. Under different circumstances however, we might expect better system performance through the creation of job conditions which are less favorable from a social and psychological point of view. Within a certain technology changes can be introduced which will improve system performance, while at the same time contributing to a deterioration in the social and psychological conditions of work. Simple changes like speed-ups and de-manning programs fit into this category. An optimum 'fit' between social and technical organization might well exist under all circumstances with respect to system performance. No guarantees exist however that this 'fit' necessarily leads to better social and psychological conditions. The implicit recognition that jobs designed to optimize system performance also meet best the psychological and social needs of the worker obviously is a fallacy against which one must carefully guard himself. Here too, the simple formula that what is good for the organization is good for the people does not hold under all conditions.

The recommended changes in job design rest upon unproven assumptions regarding human needs at work and a certain type of work attachment. No attempt has been made to validate the psychological job requirements and to prove the existence of the need for self-actualization among a substantial segment of the work force. Validation is complicated by the fact that 'some needs cannot always be judged from their conscious expression' (Thorsrud, 1973, 7). Silverman (1970, 123) formulates the weakest element in the approach as the 'failure of its proponents to discuss adequately the sources of the orientations of members of organizations'. Research in the U.K. (Goldthorpe et al., 1969) and the U.S. (reported in Fein, 1973a) shows clearly that the type of work attachment found among the Durham miners in the early Tavistock studies is not prevalent among all groups of industrial workers. The strong emphasis on social and psychological needs leads to the theoretical neglect of economic and security needs. This one sided focus at needs also leaves phenomena other than needs (e.g. demands) outside the theoretical framework. The theory would gain substantially in value by assigning a more relative position to the social and psychological needs, which would make the existence of economic and security needs more explicit.

The absence of the wage system and the role of the trade union in the theoretical framework results directly from the above described emphasis on the social and psychological needs. Most wage systems are directly connected with the job design and work loads. The union role is particularly important in the crafts and in U.S. industrial relations in general, where the existence of vested worker interests in work rules is laid down in detailed union-management contracts.

The 'open socio-technical system' theory is built on a large number of value premises which never can be verified. Autonomy in work, interdependence, and self-involvement are taken for granted as social goods and positive human values in their own right.

The positive aspects of group work are well documented in the Tavistock publications, however problems of group conformity and the danger of social isolates are completely neglected. A strong loyalty towards group norms is assumed. Small group research (Shaw, 1971) has made an important contribution to our understanding of group conformity. The problematic position of isolated group members is also reported from experiments with autonomous work groups (Den Hertog and Kerkhoff, 1973). No specific directions are provided about how to cope with these negative consequences of the introduction of autonomous grousp.

No boundaries are identified outside which the introduction of groups is technically impossible. The research of Burbidge (1974) seems to indicate that work group experiments are limited to certain technologies. Out of 329 applications surveyed by Burbidge 312 were applications under assembly (98) and component processing technologies (214). Certain boundaries for the application of work groups need therefore to be specified.

The start of a continuous change process which is often referred to in the works of the AFI can easily be halted through a number of barriers. Inadequate attention is given to the conditions which might support such a larger change process. A crucial barrier neglected in the AFI approach are the power differences between the various interest groups within an organization. The integrative nature of the system approach leads to a logical neglect of this power factor within organizations.

As is clear from the presented evaluation of the 'open socio-technical system' approach; it is an approach, and certainly not an adequate theory of job design. To underline and clarify some of the theoretical weaknesses of the approach it was briefly regarded as a theory, but it can much better be described as a set of prescriptions or guidelines with respect to the nature of the design process and the redesigned job itself. The application of the approach requires distinct technological and worker characteristics. Both technology and worker attachment to work must be suitable to the work group process. Practice indicates that technology is not so manipulable as assumed in the Tavistock approach. Also the approach is not fully neutral in its value perspective. The system notion with system performance as its main dependent variable has a bias in the direction of the management efficiency interests.

If we look at the practice of job redesign within the context of the Norwegian Cooperation Projects however, it must be recognized that this practice compensates for many of the theoretical shortcomings. The introduction of worker participation into the design and change process indicates an acceptance of the fact that in most instances the 'fit' between technology and social organization is not that optimal from the workers' point of view. The injection of worker and union influence is necessary to safeguard not only the social and psychological, but also the economic needs of the work force subject to a redesign of their jobs. In practice the wage system becomes a central element in the redesign process. Under technologies other than process and assembly, changes are introduced which differ from the autonomous group notion. The contribution of the Norwegian researchers to the field of job design does not in the first place lie with their theoretical notions but in their practical approach of supplementing and implementing many of the Tavistock ideas. Application of the Tavistock ideas themselves in no way guarantees any increase in influence of the workers. Unilaterally introduced changes in job design can hardly be expected to contribute to democracy at the shop floor of an undertaking. The link with democratization processes can only be established by providing for worker control over the redesign process. The success of the experiments within a context of industrial democracy depends on the extent the workers are *adequately represented* and *actually control* the design process. The opening up of this process to workers is a major contribution of Thorsrud to the earlier notions of the Tavistock Institute. The openendedness of the approach, earlier listed as an advantage, provides some difficulties for worker participation. The ambiguity and uncertainty inherent in the approach combined with its difficult terminology makes translation into more common concepts a first prerequisite.

Finally the criticisms against the lack of objectivity and value freeness in the approach is only applicable if one accepts the possible existence of a value free and objective job design approach. I happen to reject the notion of a value free approach and underwrite Cherns' argument that psychologists and social scientists working in this area 'have misled themselves that their approach was value free and objective, and so they have done less to advance the cause of human values in work than they might have done had they accepted the inevitability of a value laden approach" (Cherns, 1973, 27). The descriptive research that is conducted tends to support the status quo in current job design and does not point to alternative designs based on different value perspectives. The humanistic researchers have indicated that all social research is normative because 'the social universe is not a given in the same sense as a physical universe' (Argyris, 1973, 160). The former is a construction by man, which can be reconstructed if deemed necessary. Research based on humanistic assumptions can provide us with alternatives which can only be properly evaluated if segments of our work force have actually experienced these alternatives. Of course 'it requires the eye of faith' (Fox, 1971, 13) to strive for self-actualization in work for large segments of our work force. Limited experimentation so far has showed however that improvements in job content and working conditions can actually be achieved at 'costs' acceptable to management. I accept the humanistic value premises underlying the work of Thorsrud and his collaborators, who advocate more interesting and stimulating jobs under better working conditions. Putting adequate controls in the hands of the workers involved should safeguard against a possible domination of these partly academic and intellectual values. Democracy at the shop floor through job redesign can only become effective if it emerges in a democratic form, which seems to be a tautology but most democratic reforms and systems of participation have been imposed by managerial, intellectual, or political elites. The attempt to reconcile both worker and management interests into one approach must be evaluated positively, this despite the fact that there will be continuing disagreement about the nature of the 'true' worker interest and the 'best' way to achieve this interest.

4. Evaluation of the cooperation project

OVERVIEW

The development of the research design — data base — evaluation criteria — the four demonstration companies — Norsk Medisinal Depot — reasons for limited diffusion in Norway — intra company spreading — the role of the trade union — organizational change and the environment — national impact of the Cooperation Project — conclusions.

The evaluation of the Norwegian field projects in job redesign is preceeded by a research chronicle, a subsequent discussion of the data material and the manner in which it was gathered.

The original research design for the evaluation of the Norwegian Cooperation Project was a concurrent type of design. Standardized research instruments mainly taken from the organizational psychology literature were selected in order to assess differences between experimental and non-experimental plants. The key independent variable was the extent of worker autonomy in the immediate job setting; individual job satisfaction and productivity were the major dependent variables. An additional dependent variable was the workers perceived amount of control over their own destiny. It was hypothesized that workers in the experimental plants would score higher on this measure than workers in plants where no experimentation had taken place. Before my departure to Norway from the United States the questionnaires were translated into Norwegian and the nature of my task in Norway was pretty well specified. This planned research emphasized mainly individual variables and only minor attention was given to process elements and the institutional and industrial relations contexts of the Norwegian job design experiments.

Upon my arrival at the Work Research Institutes in Oslo I quickly discovered that my planned type of research was not very well received by the Institutes' senior researchers who preferred a much more action oriented process type of social science research. Two general objections were expressed against my proposed research design:

1. Data gathered through standardized survey research instruments do not have much meaning and validity without detailed knowledge of the com-

panies and the interaction processes inside the companies in which these instruments are used.
2. Survey type of research is highly inadequate for capturing organizational process information.

In addition there was a desire from the side of the AFI-researchers not to burden the experimental companies with a questionnaire study which was of little value to the management of the companies and to the workers participating in the experiments. Alternative inroads into these companies were not readily available, in particular because the Cooperation Council had recently sent a simple questionnaire to those companies which are active in the area of job redesign.

These criticisms and reactions to my proposed research design forced me to examine much that I had previously taken for granted or ignored. The limitations of the traditional social science research paradigm from a perspective of social change became very clear to me. My exposure to practical company problems in the area of job design underlined that in dealing with these problems one cannot tease out separate psychological, sociological, economic or technological bits, because practical problems always involve working with a totally integrated organizational unit. Redesigning individual jobs and larger organizations requires a multi-disciplinary approach in which linkages are established between the behavioral and the physical sciences (Herbst, 1974(a)).

These conditions made it necessary to completely rethink my research design and my role as a social scientist. The traditional aim of social science is the development of a theory. After the construction and the testing of the theory, the data and the persons from whom the data are obtained are looked at as dispensible after use. Also the use and the beneficiaries of social science research are often defined outside the realm of interest and responsibility of the social scientist. Herbst (1974(c)) advocates a cooperative relation between researcher and organization with as ultimate goal the building of a research capacity into the organization itself. The product of this type of social science research is not a new theory but a process. The establishment of a research capacity within an organization is a point of departure for the exploration of further possibilities of organizational development. The need for new theories will constantly arise as a result of the ongoing change processes in the organization.

For this type of action research the survey study is of very limited use. Survey studies if longitudinal can identify changes in attitudes, organizational structures and other selected criteria. Covariance between variables and prediction of outcomes can be established under certain conditions. However the scientific ability to predict is not a sufficient condition for implementing organizational change programs. Prediction should be accompanied by an understanding of the change processes themselves. The traditional social science research methods, using standardized research instruments, are inadequate in capturing these important social processes. In addition the construct validity of so many social science instruments leave much to be desired. If the measurements of social phenomena are inadequate, even the most sophisticated and advanced procedures of data analysis will not yield explanations (Phillips, 1973).

In my research I have attempted to complement the dominant social science paradigm by presenting an in-depth case study of the Norwegian experiments in job design. The weaknesses of this type of study are evident, however I hope to contribute to the understanding of the many factors which impinge on organizational change processes. By doing so I hopefully also will stimulate the readers' interest in change processes which lead to more democratic forms of organization.

During my 18 months stay in Norway, data on which the evaluation presented here is based were collected from the following sources:

1. More than 50 interviews were conducted with people who in some or another manner were involved with the projects. These interviews include visits to six companies where experiments were underway. In addition, I was in continuous contact with several researchers at the AFI.
2. Participation in a number of job design seminars organized by NAF in collaboration with LO. These seminars are specially designed for companies which are preparing change programs in this area. Both management and union representatives of 12 companies attended these seminars.
3. Evaluation reports which are available in Norwegian. Three specific evaluation studies do exist: Thorsrud and Emery's (1970*) report on the four demonstration companies, a report prepared by the Cooperation Council LO-NAF (Samarbeidsradet, 1973*), and an evaluation study authored by a number of researchers from the AFI (Gulowsen et al. 1973*).
4. A large number of published and unpublished reports from field experiments written by AFI researchers. Some of the more known reports are Thorsrud and Emery (1970*), Engelstad (1970*), Gulowsen (1971*, 1972, 1974*), and Karlsen (1972).

In addition to these reports other sources which provided valuable information were a considerable number of papers presented by researchers, LO, NAF, and government representatives at a variety of conferences and meetings. Also extensive use was made of documents from LO, NAF, and the Cooperation Council. Using these sources the following general picture emerges.

Information was available from about 36 companies which in varying degrees have been participating in some form of job redesign. These 36 companies actually include about 42 research sites in which some activities have taken place. These figures however give a strongly inflated impression of the actual data base. The most detailed information is available about the initial 4 demonstration companies: Christiania Spigerverk, Hunsfos, Nobø, and Norsk Hydro. These four companies started experimentation in the 1964-1968 period and the general idea was that they should provide clear examples which could be followed by other Norwegian companies in the later diffusion phase. The remaining 32 companies represent a very heterogeneous group. Only 5 of these companies have been able to start a change process over which some agreement exists that important changes have taken place and that the change process is still continuing. Another 14 companies are in a rather preliminary phase in which either preparations for change are being made or where initial changes at the shop floor have only recently taken place. The remaining 13 companies either had planned a change program but never actucally implemented it, or changes at the shop floor did take place, but the change process was halted for one or another reason after a relatively short period of time. These numbers show that the diffusion of the job design ideas within Norwegian industry over a six year period (1968-1974) has been altogether disappointing. The Cooperation Council evaluates the spreading as follows: 'The interest in starting local cooperation projects can only be evaluated as absolutely minimal given the publicity the Cooperation Project has gotten' (Samarbeidsradet, 1973*, 25).

At the time of this writing, the Fall of 1974, probably a few more companies were active in this area but no detailed information about their activities was available. Table 9 represents one possible grouping of the 36 companies. This table is an attempt to bring some order in this heterogeneous group of companies using criteria which are generally accepted as relevant in Norway. My evaluation of the Cooperation Project restricts itself only to companies in the manufacturing and service sectors. Diffusion from the original 4 demonstration companies has also taken place to the shipping and education sectors, but these developments fall outside the scope of my analysis.

Before goin into the discussion of possible evaluation criteria two issues merit attention: the character of the diffusion strategy and the lack of hard data that exists for evaluation purposes. The latter could be a possible result of the diffusion strategy. From the very beginning Thorsrud presented his ideas as non-ideological and serving both management and worker interests. Productivity was explicitly downplayed as an important factor in the job design experiments. This strategy was selected in order to gain acceptance for the job design ideas in both management and labor circles. However, this neutral position with respect to management and worker interests also creates ambiguity. In Sweden the employers' association has chosen an alternative strategy and 'sells' the new job design notions as advanced methods to improve productivity and organization flexibility (see e.g. Lindestad and Norstedt, 1973).[1] NAF in Norway has been much more careful in its attitude. It fears that too strong an emphasis by the employers on the productivity aspects of job design might result in an antagonistic union attitude. Even despite the slow diffusion in Norway, Skard (NAF) stated that NAF 'reluctantly will take the risk that a cooperation project is perceived within companies as essentially a management device which serves management interests' (Skard, 1973*, 9-10). It could be that hard data does not serve this 'neutral' diffusion strategy. It is somewhat surprising in my opinion that neither LO nor NAF is engaged in any evaluation work. The evaluation report prepared by the Cooperation Council (Samarbeidsradet, 1973*) certainly lacks hard data. In addition, the strong emphasis by the researchers on the process aspects of the change projects could explain a lack of interest in standard measures like absenteeism, turnover, productivity etc.[2] The only report that attempts some kind of systematic evaluation is Gulowsen et al. (1973*). Unfortunately this otherwise excellent report also lacks operating statistics from the experiments.

One outstanding characteristic of the Cooperation Project is that the parties participating in it all have different motivations for their participation and even more important have different perceptions of what the most important elements of the Project are. The implication for evaluation is a long list of possible criteria which can be used in appraising the job design experiments in individual companies. Which are the major parties involved in the

1. The lower degree of labor-management cooperation in most Swedish experiments makes what is spreading there essentially different from Thorsrud's job design approach as presented in the previous chapter.
2. This is not to argue that these standard measures are necessarily the best criteria for evaluation of the projects. They do provide however supplementary information which is generally accepted as important.

Table 9. Companies' participation in cooperation project (Fall 1974).

Demonstration companies (4)	Substantial changes have been accomplished and project is continuing (5)	Companies which are in planning or early implementation phase (14)	Planned project, but it never started or failed in early implementation phase (13)
Christiania Spigerverk	Hotel Calendonien	Søyland	Trondhjem Mek. Verksted
Hunsfos (3)*	Norsk Medisinaldepot	Dyna	Grorud
Norsk Hydro (4)	Norsk Shell	Øgland	Treschow Fritzøe
Nobø (2)	Siemens	Jordan	Per Schøyen
	Block Wattne	Lilleborg	Harrald Møller
		Borregaard	Bjarne Wist
		Myrens Verksted	Vittingfoss
		Tiedemanns	Blikkvalsverket
		Ardal	Fonas
		Roggaland	Norsk Neffelin
		Høie	Nosted Bruk
		Knekten	Aukra Bruk
		Falconbridge Nikkel	Sem
		National Trykkeriet	

* Between brackets number of research sites.

Cooperation Project, what is their main reason for participation and which criteria do they use in evaluating the developments so far? Six major parties can be identified here for my purposes: NAF (the national employers' federation), LO (the national trade union federation), the management of a company, the local union, the shop floor workers, and the researchers involved. The general position of these six groups can be briefly described as follows:

NAF. In the early sixties NAF supported the Cooperation Project for two main reasons: 1. the experiments in job redesign were perceived as a preferable alternative to board representation as a method to increase industrial democracy within the firm. NAF hoped that the experiments at least would delay the introduction of the latter form to further industrial democracy. 2. The new forms of work organization as advocated by Emery and Thorsrud were expected to make better use of human resources, to contribute to economic growth, and to raise the competitiveness of Norwegian industry. The passage of the 1972 legislation makes the first motivation clearly irrelevant today and the number of experiments has been too small to contribute significantly to the second objective. In the last five years NAF has changed its views on the experiments and today they are more perceived as an important tool to improve labor-management cooperation at the shop floor. NAF rejects the connection between shop floor changes and necessary adaptions in the power structure of the larger organization. Skard formulates NAF's position on this issue as follows: 'What is really happening is that the principle of the delegation of authority is applied in a new way' (Skard, 1973, 9). The issue of productivity is clearly downplayed by NAF. Too strong an emphasis on productivity might antagonize the unions, it is feared.

LO. The LO endorsed the Cooperation Project in the early sixties because of its potential to: 1. increase industrial democary within the undertaking; 2. reduce alienation of the individual worker; and 3. increase productivity which is beneficial for all workers. Over the years LO's position towards the projects has been ambivalent. More recently however stronger supports is given to them. Now they are perceived as efforts to improve the conditions under which the individual worker has to work. This includes giving the worker more autonomy in his task. From a broader perspective job redesign and related shop floor changes can increase the workers' influence within the undertaking and they are in a way complementary to the more traditional methods to wield influence like collective bargaining, the shop steward, the work council, the corporate assembly and the representation on the board (Halverson, Hansen, and Aspengren, all in personal interviews, Fall 1974).

Management. The local employer is very pragmatic in his reasoning whether or not to start a change program at the shop floor level. In most cases he will initiate a project as a response to a specific managerial problem e.g. high turnover and inability to attract sufficient labor, inadequate flexibility of the work force, overall bad management-labor relations, or low productivity. Employers generally are not interested in starting an overall change program but react to a specific problem situation they are faced with.

Union Local. Generally the union reacts to a management initiative in this area. Out of the 32 companies listed in Table 9 (excluding the 4 demonstration companies) only 4 experiments were started on union, work-council or combined labor-management initiative.Through a job redesign project the union in many cases tries to further its more traditional objectives like higher wages, changes in the wage system, upgrading and equalizing work conditions at the plant level.

Workers. Most often workers play a waiting game in the early phases of an experiment. Management and the union have to build a necessary trust level before workers start actively engaging themselves. Higher wages through skill increases and more interesting work seem to be the important aspects for the workers. There exists however only fragmentary data about why workers participate in the job redesign projects.

Researchers. The aim of the researchers has been to generate 'a long term strategy for social and technological change' (Gustavsen, 1974, 1). The Cooperation Project was seen as the start of a larger organizational and societal change process by improving the conditions for personal participation at the shop floor level. At a more immediate level the researchers aimed at increasing the level of autonomy and selfregulation and create opportunies for individual learning at work (Gulowsen et al., 1974*).

It is obvious that the parties participating in the project have quite different motivations and perceptions of the project. These differences however do not keep the parties from cooperating and the issue of job design is clearly perceived as an issue of an integrative nature (see Chapter 1). In the words of former LO secretary Halverson: 'Even if the parties may have different fundamental motivations for participating in such projects both parties have deemed it useful to collaborate in the Cooperation Project' (Halverson, 1971, 3). The main criteria used by the different groups can now be summarized and a rather crude indication is given to what extent these criteria have been met in the experiments:

NAF	better labor-management cooperation	?
	higher productivity	+
LO	increased workers' influence in direct task	+
	increased workers' influence in wider management	—
Management	reduced turnover/absenteeism	+
	attract sufficient labor	?
	increased flexibility	+
	higher productivity	+
Union Local	higher wages	+
	changes in wage system	+
	upgrading	+
Workers	higher wages	+
	upgrading	+
	more interesting work	+
Researchers	start of larger change process	?
	major changes in technology	—
	increased worker autonomy	+
	more opportunities for learning	+[3]

This crude evaluation gives a rather positive general picture. Taking the companies individually reveals however a more heterogeneous picture. In the individual cases wide differences exist in the extent to which the above listed criteria are met. A preliminary conclusion can be that given certain local conditions most criteria can be met and do not seem to be mutually exclusive.

What has actually happened within the individual companies? Thorsrud describes the typical features of a change program as:

a. Multi-skilling of operators so that they can alternate between different work roles inside partly autonomous work groups. This is usually needed because of the prevalent philosophy of one man- one skill.
b. Development of the measures of variations and of the data analysis methods needed for control by the operators. This is often necessary because control has been traditionally held at a level which is too removed to undertake quick and detailed control action and hence has not needed the requisite information. In one case the establishment of a new information room was a major part during one phase of an experiment.
c. Attachment of a local repair man to back up the quick and detailed control actions for which the operators are expected to assume responsibility.

3. This evaluation is based on the data sources listed on pages 50, and 51, of this chapter.

d. Institutionalizing the meetings, contacts, etc. that enable the operators, as a group, to plan and coordinate their activities.
e. Training the foremen to supervise, coordinate and plan for the activities of groups rather than individuals. This usually means an extension of their time-span of responsibility and some skilling in tasks of appraisal diagnosis and planning of production that are traditionally located at middle management level.
f. Design and introduction of new bonus arrangement if the department has or needs some special kind of incentive schemes.

(Thorsrud, 1972, 44-45; also in Thorsrud and Emery, 1970*, 216-218).

My analysis which follows will particularly focus at the industrial relations aspects of these changes. The technical aspects of job redesign are partly treated in the preceding chapter. Much more technical information about the change process is available in addition to that presented here.[4] Many people are working on the technical aspects and it is mainly for this reason that these aspects of job design are here only presented in a rather sketchy manner. In order to provide a full picture of the nature of the Cooperation Project the four demonstration companies will be discussed first. These four companies were selected by the researchers in cooperation with representatives from LO and NAF. The type of technology and the potential for diffusion were important criteria in the selection of three of the four companies. Norsk Hydro was not actually selected but its top management asked to participate in the project. This was granted mainly because the great prestige of Norsk Hydro within Norwegian industry.

Christiania Spigerverk[5]

The first experiment in the Cooperation Project was started in this metal manufacturing company in 1964. Christiania Spigerverk is located in Oslo and employs some 1200 workers. The wire drawing department was chosen as the experimental area among others because the low morale and relative high turnover of the employees. Thorsrud (1971, 50-51) aptly describes the type of work in the wire drawing department:

'Thick wire is run at a very high speed through a set of reducing dies, finally emerging in a thin coil which is bundled away. The machinery required is designed in such a way that

4. The references used for the individual companies provide the interested reader with a good start.
5. This section draws heavily upon Thorsrud and Emery (1970*), Thorsrud (1971) and Karlsen (1972).

the supervision and handling involved is seen as a one-man job. Engineers, although they have a choice in the design of the machinery, usually seem to favour the one requiring this sort of organization, i.e. one man in charge. But an examination of the workload involved shows the following pattern: most of the time the man is literally doing nothing, in fact he is probably sitting down reading a comic or paper behind his bench and out of sight of anyone else. Then suddenly the wire breaks, and he is working flat out; it is really a two-man job to get it back on, but he is the only man available. There is some handling and inspection, and a little welding, but basically the pattern of activities fails to meet the criteria of optimal workload and variety.'

To change this pattern of work the researchers proposed to alter the one-man/one-machine pattern into a work organization whereby a group of workers took responsibility for a group of machines. Before introduction of the changes a number of guarantees were agreed upon between the local union and management. Briefly these guarantees were:

1. No changes in manning. The seven wire drawing benches chosen for the experiment should be manned by the same number of workers as required under the traditional work organization.
2. A guaranteed minimum wage was agreed upon which was approximately 1% above the average earnings for the preceding four weeks. An incentive was established if the experimental group would produce above the average level of the preceding 4 weeks.
3. The workers who participated should be volunteers. It was the task of the shop steward to recruit these volunteers.

Despite these guarantees and the strong support of the local union the workers in the experimental area were rather indifferent to the project. The project was generally perceived more as relating to the national goals set up by LO and NAF for the experiments than to a learning and change program at the local level (Thorsrud, 1971, 52). Also there was evidence of a lack of trust by the workers of their union leadership and management. 'The men just could not believe that they were not being sold down the river by their union leadership and management – more work for less money' (Thorsrud, 1971, 51). In the early phase it also appeared that the workers who were to participate, were not at all volunteers. 'Partly, they had been persuaded by trade union leaders, partly they wanted to avoid being removed from the machines where they habitually worked and where the experiments would take place. It appeared that the local shop steward committee experienced serious difficulties in marshalling its members. A critical situation arose when one worker refused to participate and at the same time refused to be moved from the experimental area' (Thorsrud, 1970, 76).

When the experiment finally got underway, a group of workers became responsible for a group of machines, the researchers ran into another unexpected problem: how to deal with the extra productivity generated by this group method of working. Productivity increased with about 20 percent but if the workers in the experimental area were given fair payment for this additional production they would then be among the highest paid employees of the plant. This was clearly unacceptable for the other employees for whom there were no productivity increases to justify increases in wages. The workers in the wire mill then proposed to be paid by additional leisure. This however was resisted both by management and NAF. During the experimental period satisfaction among the workers increased and the greater freedom provided by the group system was generally appreciated. After half a year the researchers withdrew from the field side and because management was unable to apply the new working methods on a larger scale and could not deal with the productivity problems, the work organization in the wire mill was changed back to the traditional set-up.

Christiania Spigerverk was for the Norwegian researchers a very important first case where they could test some of their design principles and gain practical experience in this area. For the purposes of this analysis the Christiania Spigerverk project identified three very important issues in the area of job redesign:

1. Job redesign and the wage system are highly intertwined. The existing wage system, which was unable to deal with the productivity increases, was clearly the most important factor that contributed to the stagnation of the project. In addition the project showed that wage increases can only be tolerated within fairly narrow socially defined limits. Exceeding these limits will result in strong reactions from other groups (the issue of coercive comparisons).

2. There did exist initial worker resistance against the proposed changes. General lack of trust and concern about changes in the established 'work-effort bargain'[6] make a formal agreement which guarantees no changes in manning and maintenance of wages a necessary condition for an experiment to be accepted by the workers.

6. The work-effort bargain reflects the 'accepted' amount of work to be done for a given wage. According to Behrend (1957, 505) 'every employment contract (whatever the method of wage payment) consists of two elements: 1. an agreement on the wage rate (either per unit of time or per unit of output), i.e. a wage rate bargain; and 2. an agreement on the work to be done, i.e. an effort bargain'. This latter bargain is generally implicit and imprecise, resting on predominantly intuitive norms like a 'fair day's work'.

3. The experiment represented a successful application of the group form of work organization, however the new organization could not maintain itself in a larger structure organized on different principles. A continuous change process certainly did not develop.

Hunsfos[7]

The Hunsfos pulp and paper mill, the fifth largest mill in Norway, is located in a small community in the very South of Norway. Hunsfos is the major employer in this community and employed in 1963 almost 50% of the local adult male working population. The factory is highly integrated with the community and many workers' parents and grandparents were also employed by this company. The local community has many 'gemeinschaft' characteristics. Work life is closely linked to religious, political and economic life of the community. The local trade union fits the same model of a high degree of integration with the community. Top management of Hunsfos is probably a little paternalistic in its general orientation towards the employees. The predominant technology in the pulp and paper production is process technology. Hunsfos was facing economic problems in the early 1960's, mainly caused by a general difficult position of the whole Norwegian pulp and paper industry. It was this economic position that made management decide to start a job redesign project in 1964. From the very beginning the local union had a positive attitude towards the project probably because it realized that something had to be done in order to save many jobs at Hunsfos.

Management, the union, and the researchers together selected the chemical pulp department as the first experimental area. This area was mainly selected because of the process technology and its expected strategic position for diffusion of possible results to the company as a whole. A very detailed socio-technical analysis of this department was made by Engelstad. Among others the following problems were identified:

1. An inadequate wage system. The total wage of an operator consisted of hourly pay, shift allowances, regular overtime, additional hours and production bonus. This complexity may it almost impossible for the individual worker to see any direct relationship between his efforts and wages.

7. This section is mainly based upon Engelstad (1970*, 1972) and Thorsrud and Emery (1970*).

The production bonus was based upon quantity of output over which the worker had only minimum control. In contrast the quality of the product, which was very important to management could be controlled by the workers but was not incorporated in the bonus.

2. The difficult position of the foreman. A shift foreman was introduced after a recent change-over to a new production method. The foreman's main task was to deal with the problems resulting from this change-over. The foreman, who was selected from the ranks of the operators, developed the 'practice of being constantly on the move as a troubleshooter within the department; he would then do most of the unpredictable tasks that the operators were reluctant to carry out without special compensations perceiving such tasks as falling outside their own strictly defined jobs' (Engelstad, 1972, 342). This behavior had the effect that the job content of the operators became more and more reduced. Engelstad (1972, 342) summarizes this problem as 'By filling in for their subordinates, the managers and foremen were subtly redefining their own jobs in a way that reinforced the tendencies of the men on the shop floor not to show more initiative than was demanded by the traditional design'.

3. The problem with segregated jobs. The training of operators for only one specialized task under process technology makes it very difficult to cope with variances in the production process. Highly specialized tasks are positive from a training and supervisory point of view, but it is by now well documented that workers tend to react to such specialization by interpreting their job specification as the maximum they owe rather than the minimum. Disruptions under process production can better be handled by multi-skilled operators who have some kind of understanding of the total process. This multi-skilling opens up the possibility of upgrading for the workers and a work organization that provides more flexibility.

After the detailed analysis the following specific measures were introduced in order to create a work group with responsibility for the total production process:

'1. Training the operators to make them as far as possible qualified for all taks within the department.
2. Allocation of a special repairman to the operator group to cope with smaller break-downs requiring immediate attention.
3. Setting up an information center on the shop floor where measurements and other information were quickly available so that everyone would be aware of the current situation in the department.

4. Arranging suitable conditions for department employees to meet in smaller or larger groups when necessary.
5. Installation of telephones in each department section.
6. Electing a group representative on each shift to facilitate communication'.
(Engelstad, 1972, 346).

In addition a new marginal group bonus was introduced based on output quality. The whole process from the start of the experiment in 1964 to the actual introduction of the first changes in January 1966 took more than 15 months. The union was very supportive of the ideas despite the fact that in the Norwegian pulp and paper industry the number of operator positions and their functions are strictly prescribed in the collective agreement between management and the union. The positive role of subsequent active shop stewards at Hunsfos cannot be underestimated. This support was clearly required, there 10 out of 15 of the senior operators in the experimental department were over 50 years of age. A first vote whether or not to start an experiment was carried with the smallest possible margin 15 in favor, 14 against. It was the support of the local shop steward and local plant management that led to workers agreeing in the proposed changes. Engelstad (1970*, 144) reports that the local union shop stewards gave the following reasons for this narrow margin in favor of an experiment:

1. The historical mistrust of management was only very recently reinforced by new measures to reduce cost in the chemical pulp department. A transfer of some workers to other departments had been a part of these measures.
2. In the beginning the project was perceived as being dominated by management and was expected to lead only to 'reduced manning and increased work effort'. The researchers were also perceived as management oriented.
3. A lack of confidence in the abilities of the shop stewards to effectively protect the worker interests in this area.
4. The workers with a little higher status in the department and with considerable autonomy in their work did not feel any need for change in the work organization.

The experiment itself considerably changed the mood of the workers and a vote after one year whether or not to continue the change process was carried in favor of the project with only a few workers against. In addition to the change in attitudes among the workers the new work organization also led to increased quality of the pulp production and a higher production level.

After 1967 experiments were started in other production areas. Top management's commitment to the changes (Jarlsby, 1973*) was critical in diffusing the ideas to other departments. Hunsfos is about the only company in Norway where the job design ideas have very slowly spread throughout the company. In other departments the same initial worker resistance had to be dealt with but in later phases it was obvious that the workers did not want to return to the old work organization. Elden and Engelstad give the following brief chronology of the project at Hunsfos:

'1. Socio-technical analysis on company level and selection of the experimental site (1964).
2. First experiment in the chemical pulp department (1965-1967).
3. Clarification of company and union policy with respect to the chemical pulp department resulting in a joint agreement on project continuation (1967).
4. Second experiment in paper machines No. 3 and No. 4 (1968-1969).
5. Clarification of company and union policy with respect to the experiments in the paper machines resulting in joint agreement to extend project activities to all production departments (1969).
6. Information activities in all departments and development and introduction of a new combined worker-training program and payment system (1970-1972).'

(Elden and Engelstad, 1973, 5).

This chronology reflects the slow but continuous change process at Hunsfos. No definite stagnation occurred and changes slowly diffused through the Hunsfos pulp and paper mill. Almost eight years of slowly progressing work in job redesign at Hunsfos does not seem to contribute to a more active interest among workers in the other forms to increase industrial democracy within their company. In elections for the corporate assembly only 32% of the Hunsfos workers participated. This figure compares very unfavorable to the workers' turnout for this election in comparable firms also organized by the National Union of Paper Industry Workers. For seven comparable firms the turnout figures were respectively 78%, 74%, 70%, 65%, 60%, and 52% (Fri Fagbewegelse, 1973*, 10, 1). The low turnout at Hunsfos does not seen to support the assumption that increased autonomy at work will contribute to greater personal involvement in other democratic processes.[8] In 1974 the local union complained that the change processes were not developing fast enough and that further progress only could be made by changing the middle management roles. The union demanded to know exactly what top manage-

---

8. The local union however was considerably strengthened as a result of the experiments. Hunsfos became almost 100% organized and the new union strength was reflected in a more active union posture on a wide range of issues.

ment's ideas were concerning further extension of influence of the workers. The Hunsfos case identified the following main issues:

1. Initial worker resistance can be overcome by strong union support. The Hunsfos case provides clear support for what can be called the 'experience hypothesis'. This hypothesis can be formulated as follows: Despite initial resistance to change, workers do not want to go back to the old form of work organization after they have worked under the new system for a period of time.
2. The role of the foreman can become very problematic if many new responsibilities are given to the work group. Transfer to a new position or changes in the foreman role can be possible solutions.
3. Existing job regulations can be overcome under conditions of good labor-management relations.
4. Top management and union support is necessary for further organizational spreading.
5. Over a period of about 8 years job design ideas slowly spread to other departments. Within individual departments however a stagnation point was reached when further changes required alteration of the lower and middle management roles.

Nobø[9]

In 1965 Nobø management turned to the researchers and suggested an experiment in its Hommelvik department where a new production line for electrical heaters was set up. At the time of the experiment Nobø was a fast growing company with stable and progressive labor-management relations. The Hommelvik plant had a work force of about 100 persons. In 1965 the production of a new panel heater was started and about 30 men and women were initially employed in this new section. There were no foremen in the plant. Two 'contact persons', who did not receive extra pay, took care of the necessary communication between workers and management. The technology consisted of two different production lines which were split up in simple, specialized, and repetitive jobs designed through the use of traditional work studies and Method Time Measurements (MTM).

The basic changes in job design were rather straight forward. The produc-

9. Based upon Qvale in Karlsen (1972), Gulowsen et al. (1973*), Thorsrud and Emery (1970*).

tion lines ultimately were split up in five different sections each covering one of the main stages of production. Five work groups involving 110 workers were organized with responsibility for the production of specified parts of the heaters. Job rotation within each group and to some extent between groups was started by workers themselves. Brief planning sessions were held each morning for the three work groups for coordination and planning purposes. Flexibility of the work groups was increased because the operators were able to perform more than one job. Productivity was satisfactory and turnover and absenteeism compared favorably with other Nobø plants. In a later phase of the experiment the incentive part of the wage system was reduced from 40% to 5%. In short, the Nobø experiment seemed to be rather successful from a job design point of view.

In 1971 Nobø closed down the electric heater department at Hommelvik and started up production in a new factory in a neighboring community. Managers from the company's headquarters were mainly responsible for the work organization in this new factory which provided the workers with less autonomy than in their previous jobs in the old factory. Local management and the union reacted strongly but to no avail. The conditions in the new plant deteriorated with as result that the researchers withdrew from the company. There were some indications that management was trying to use the label of the Cooperation Project to manipulate workers and introduce higher production standards and speed-ups. The local union was apparently not strong enough to fight these changes effectively.

The Nobø case provides us with another successful application of the autonomous work group idea. The main lesson that in addition must be drawn from this case is that job design experiments can be used by management to change work without any consideration for the workers involved. This manipulation is only possible when the local union is weak. The shift from one plant to another had considerably weakened the union organization in the Nobø case.

Norsk Hydro[10]

Norsk Hydro is one of Norway's biggest companies. Its main activities are in the chemical sector although very recently Norsk Hydro has become one

10. Based upon Gulowsen (1974), a number of interviews with Ryste and one interview with the Norwegian minister of Social Affairs, Halverson, who in 1966 were respectively secretary and president of the union local at the Norsk Hydro Herøya complex.

of the major companies engaged in the exploration and exploitation of the North Sea oil and gas. Total employment is around 8000. The company's big production complex is located at Herøya where about 5000 workers are employed, many of them commuters from neighboring communities. The production workers are organized by the Herøya union (HAF) which belongs to the National Union of Chemical Workers. The degree of organization is high (over 90%) and HAF has an extensive bargaining agreement with the Hydro management which goes into very much detail with respect to wages and wage related issues but is in comparison with U.S. contracts rather deficient in the area of job regulation. HAF is seen by some as one of the stronger union locals in Norway.

The start of a Cooperation Project at Norsk Hydro was very interesting because of the quite opposite motivations of management and the local union. Several Norsk Hydro factories were in 1966/1967 in a difficult economic position. Competition had increased, profits had fallen and there was a fear for security of employment among the workers. Technical and economic changes were deemed necessary to make the factories viable again. Certain factories were clearly 'overmanned'. In addition to the unfavorable economic conditions labor-management relations were also rather bad. Among the workers there was a growing fear of losing their jobs in addition to general dissatisfaction with wages which had been lagging behind the wage developments of the companies inside Hydro's 'orbit of coercive comparisons'.

In 1967 a new president was appointed at Norsk Hydro whose main task was to restore the company's profit making abilities. The new president was convinced that improving productivity would be substantially aided by better management-labor relations. On the side of the union there were strong demands for job security and higher wages. In the negotiations that followed it was agreed upon to work toward a new productivity agreement and to start an experiment in job redesign. Although it was agreed that the job design experiment and the productivity agreement should be considered independent of each other, it was obvious that from the union point of view the productivity agreement was seen as a precondition for the job design experiment.

The productivity agreement provided for an employment guarantee for the work force, a wage increase of 1 krone per hour, and reduction in manning levels by 10 to 20% through natural attrition. The department selected for job redesign was a new fertilizer production unit which was characterized by process technology, a higher than average turnover for Norsk Hydro plants, and a number of uncompromising shop stewards. The productivity of the plant was considered low. In this context Gulowsen (1974*) makes the observation that under most forms of process technology the workers have to work harder under low productivity conditions. High productivity means few interruptions in the production process and therefore only controlling functions for the workers. The jobs of the workers at this plant were highly specialized and even in the case of minor difficulties the supervisor had to be consulted. The wage system was very rigid and provided no incentive for a more flexible deployment of the 10 workers during each shift.

A steering group was established to oversee the change process. This group consisted of: a foreman of the production unit, a representative of HAF, an ex-foreman of another plant, a representative of the local personnel department, a representative of the central Norsk Hydro office, and a rechearcher from the AFI. An agreement was made to 'shelter' the experimental area from the other plants with respect to working conditions and payment system. This type of agreement makes deviations and changes from the traditional work organization and collective agreement stipulations possible in the experimental area. It also included a stipulation that the new arrangements in the experimental area should not automatically apply to other areas without the consent of Norsk Hydro management and HAF.

It surprised the researchers that in the first discussions of the work group job changes and changes in organizational structure were not the central topics. The problems of the wage system stood very central and dominated the discussions. The main issues discussed were bonuses, training, recruitment, and the wage system. Through all of those issues job design went like a red wire. Gulowsen (1974*, 34) in his evaluation states: 'the wage question had to be solved before other changes could be introduced'. The above described productivity agreement was the first step to solve this question.

Under process technology a flexible work group can only be formed if the workers have the necessary skills. The Norsk Hydro experiment was a breakthrough in that it linked training and education directly to pay in the collective agreement. This link established a financial incentive for the workers to start participating in the training programs and develop a number of skills which would enable them to work in a number of different jobs. The wage system was first set up in the experimental plant but in later years was expanded in the collective agreement to include all operating and maintenance workers at Herøya. The current contract also includes a clause that gives every worker the 'right to learn' at work. The wage system now provides five allowances for different levels of education and training. The necessary courses are provided by Norsk Hydro and one qualifies for an allowance if one has finished a particular course (estimated at about 100 hours) and is able to perform a number of jobs in addition to the job in which one started working. Table 10 presents this system more detailed. One qualifies, for example, for step 4 of the learning allowances if one has completed the four necessary courses and is able to perform at least 5 jobs in the relevant working area. In addition a group production bonus was established which is based upon operating quality and quantity criteria. The introduction of this system in the experimental plants worked surprisingly well. In one fertilizer plant before the experiment a worker mastered on the average 2.3 jobs. Two years later in the same department this average had risen to 5.4 out of a possible 9 jobs (Gulowsen, 1974*, 124).

As is the case with almost every wage system some tensions arose as the result of its implementation. The following three sources were the most important:

1. The evaluation process whether or not a worker has acquired the necessary skills to execute an additional job is difficult. In most cases the head of the production unit and the shop steward are responsible for this evaluation. This judgment becomes a very problematic issue for most shop stewards. It opens up the possibilities of favoritism. There was strong dissatisfaction among the workers with this evaluation system. Doubts existed about the promotion of some fellow workers to the higher categories.
2. The skilled tradesmen resisted the narrowing of wage differentials by process operators who had gained their skills through the company training program and not through the traditional craft procedures.
3. For those workers who took advantage of the new system after a couple of years a stagnation point was reached beyond which no progression was possible.

In the area of work organization some important changes were also made. Job rotation was made possible through multi-skilling which considerably increased the flexibility of the work group. This flexibility has clear advantages for management because in many cases a smaller group can operate the production process. For the workers this flexibility makes it possible to follow training courses during working hours and also increases their freedom in e.g. the scheduling of vacations. One way in which tasks were changed was the inclusion of maintenance work in the role of the operators. After initial resistance from the maintenance workers, who formed a separate group which operated out of a central maintenance office, these changes were implemented. The spirit of the experiment was reflected in the fact that the maintenance workers gave up their special status within the local trade union.[11] This spirit was also reflected by the rebuilding of an old fertilizer plant by a group of workers from the experimental plant. Over time however the continued presence of the foreman on the shop floor made further change impossible and the project slowly stagnated. This was reinforced by the departure of the dynamic leader and the secretary of the local union.

Table 10. Simplified presentation of Norsk hydro wage system (1973).

Shift, overtime, holiday etc. allowances		
Production bonus		4000–6000 Kr.
Learning allowances:		
1. Basic course + 2 jobs	0.25 / hour	
2. Supplementary basic course + 3 jobs	0.25 / hour	
3. Electrical instrumentation + 4 jobs	0.25 / hour	0–3000 Kr.
4. Basic chemistry + 5 jobs	0.25 / hour	
5. Chemistry course + all jobs in factory	0.50 / hour	
Qualification allowance process operator	0.50 / hour	
Allowance for the skilled trades	0.75 / hour	1000–1500 Kr.
Allowance for abnormal discomfort:		
1. Degree	1.50 / hour	
2. Degree	1.25 / hour	
3. Degree	1.00 / hour	0–3000 Kr.
4. Degree	0.75 / hour	
5. Degree	0.50 / hour	
Basic wage		30,000 Kr.

Union leadership was also at Norsk Hydro of crucial importance in the project. It was felt that further changes in the experimental plants were only possible if other departments and units would also start parallel change processes. The differences in working conditions that can be tolerated within one production complex are limited through reference and comparison processes operating between the several work groups. No general diffusion process within Norsk Hydro took place. The good financial results and the swift expansion into the oil field were more important areas for management than the area of job redesign. Gulowsen concludes his excellent and detailed eva-

11. In 1974, six years later, the maintenance workers decided to form again a separate group within the local union.

luation of the Norsk Hydro experiments as follows: 'The results show that it is possible to reach isolated, but not comprehensive gains through action research at the shop floor. Much indicates that progress will be short lived as long as the research is not supported by higher organizational levels which will enable changes in the power structure and the distribution of material privileges' (Gulowsen, 1974*, 222).

The project at Norsk Hydro highlights for my purposes the following important issues:

1. Job design projects can be used by management and union for purposes which were essentially external to the goals of the Cooperation Project.
2. The union in Norsk Hydro succeeded in getting a 'right to learn' clause into the contract and was able to integrate the learning opportunities into the wage system. The experiment had in addition crucial impact upon the expansion of the company's training and educational programs.
3. Changes in job design again were possible under process technology. No continuous change process materialized however. Neither was there any evidence of changes in the power structure at both the plant and company level.

In 1969 Emery and Thorsrud wrote a detailed report of the experiments in these four demonstration companies (Thorsrud and Emery, 1970*). This report was presented to the Cooperation Council which approved it and agreed that a diffusion of the new ideas and principles should be stimulated by LO and NAF. LO tried to limit the number of companies that would be allowed to start experimentation in the first years to eight, but this restriction did not have any practical significance because of the small number of companies that was actually interested in starting joint management-union job redesign programs. LO, NAF, and the Cooperation Council tried to stimulate the spreading of the new principles through a considerable number of seminars and the publication of relevant literature (see e.g. Samarbeidsradet, 1972*). As Table 9 (p. 53) showed, in the period 1969-1974 only 32 companies did actually start some kind of change process; only 5 of these experiments lead to substantial results which could be maintained over time. Before going into the causes of this slow spreading, one more company will be described in some detail. This company is an example where changes of a relative simple nature have taken place which are evaluated very positively by the employees.

Norsk Medisinaldepot[12]

Norsk Medisinaldepot is a state monopoly with the exclusive right to import and distribute pharmaceutical products in Norway. The Cooperation Project started at this company's warehouse in Oslo in 1972 after long preparations. The union has been involved in the project from the very beginning. It signed an agreement to cooperate with changes for the period of one year under the conditions that in this first year no changes in the wage system should take place. The employees in the warehouse are public employees and fall therefore under state wage regulations. The change process at Norsk Medisinaldepot has been slow. The project started initially with 20 employees in one section of the warehouse in 1972. After the first year the union and workers evaluated the changes positively and the project continued. In 1974 the new conditions had expanded to 82 employees in the warehouse. The total employment is about 280. The experiment was not started for productivity reasons. Productivity however has maintained itself at the same levels and the data on turnover and absenteeism indicate small improvements. In the long run a firm like Norsk Medisinaldepot is facing a critical problem: it needs highly responsible employees because of the nature of its products and in the mean time offers not very attractive warehouse type of employment. The experiment can be seen as a long term effort to improve the labor market position of the company.

The typical job of a warehouse employee consists of receiving an order in the form of a computer print-out and going through the warehouse stacks with a little hand-pushed cart to collect the required items. The average order is relatively small. The error rate in order preparation is low. This is important because many of the products being handled are drugs and medicines which are only available on prescription.

What kind of concrete changes have taken place?

1. Effectively, one managerial level was eliminated. The immediate supervisors of the warehouse employees were given different functions. This was facilitated by the fact that the company was building a new warehouse and the ex-supervisors were used in the planning of this new expansion. Autonomous groups were formed which had full responsibility for the planning of the work and the internal task assignments.

---

12. Based upon Qvale (1974*), oral presentations by Qvale and Karlsen, and visits to the company.

2. In addition the work groups did get the full responsibility for the following personnel matters:
   a. hiring of new personnel became a group task.
   b. the time clock was abolished. The workers themselves decide when their daily task is finished and some of them are allowed to go home early in case of insufficient orders. A lot of 'busy work' seems to be eliminated.
   c. the work group can give up to two days paid leave to each member if it is decided that the group member has a valid reason. Vacations and days-off are also regulated by the work group.
   d. a training and education system is developed in cooperation with the personnel department which provides the workers with upgrading possibilities.

These changes at Norsk Medisinaldepot show that it is possible to improve the general conditions of work without far reaching changes in the nature of the tasks. It is obvious that these type of changes are of a different nature than those proposed in the main body of work by Thorsrud and his collaborators. The changes in this company are important because they are developed with only minimal assistance from outside researchers and the changes now accomplished can be a very important first step in further changing the immediate work organization. The elimination of one supervisory level gave the employees more responsibility and variety in their work. These changes plus the important increased control over personnel matters and certain working conditions seem to be evaluated very positively by the workers and their union. Within each work group an internal coordinator is elected, but this function does not carry with it any higher remuneration. Norsk Medisinaldepot is presented here because it showed that many improvements can be made in the conditions of work without changing the task structure very substantially. This is important for two reasons: the issues of personnel administration and working conditions are very important to workers and can therefore be used as first steps in a change program, secondly where changes in task structure are very difficult to attain labor-management cooperation in a change program can at least lead to improvement in the here described areas.

As stated earlier the diffusion process in Norway has been very disappointing. In addition to the companies listed in Table 9 a number of companies have selected individual elements of the proposed job design approach e.g. job rotation or a change in wage system. These companies are not included here because the changes are minor and the process of introducing the changes does not follow the labor-management cooperation model which is such an integral part of the Cooperation Project. What is being spread differs from the change processes in the four demonstration companies. Gustavsen observes in this context: 'What can, however, be said is that what has been diffused has tended to differ from what was originally intended. Transformations have taken place, and among these transformations it seems as if the loss of the intended semi-political – not to say political – character of the project, is among the important aspects. From being a solution to a pressing political problem, the program has to a degree turned into solutions to problems within such fields as production engineering' (Gustavsen, 1974, 6). What is spreading slowly is not a broad organizational change process but a form of work organization that might better fit certain organizational conditions. Elements of the job design approach are spreading, not so much the approach itself. And even the spreading of the former seems rather restricted so far. The following discussion of the reasons for the restricted spreading is based upon information from the 36 companies listed in Table 9. First I will focus at the inter-company diffusion process, herafter the problems of intra-company spreading will be discussed.

Inter-company Diffusion. The main reason behind the low spreading in Norway in my opnion is that the researchers have overestimated the problems individual companies were faced with in the area of labor turnover, low motivation and dissatisfied workers. Local management will only start work in this area if there is a perceived problem. Certain tolerance limits have to be exceeded before management takes action. As indicated earlier over 90% of the experiments were initiated by management. The conditions in the late sixties and early seventies were not of such a character that provided management with sufficient reasons to undertake action.

This argument seems to be confirmed by the increased interest in the last year for job redesign. The expansion of the oil and oil related industries has made the labor market much tighter, creating a problem for management in a number of companies. Eleven out of twelve companies currently participating in a NAF job design seminar mentioned the labor market problem[13] (the difficulty of attracting and maintaining an adequate work force) as the basic reason why they were present at this seminar. The conditions within

13. Labor market problems also seem the main reason for the faster spreading in Sweden. The new Volvo Kalmar plant was only built because management could not 'afford' a traditional automobile plant given the Swedish labor market situation (Gyllenhammer, 1974).

the companies in the years between 1968-1973 were not such that management was forced to undertake action in this area. This lack of motivation on the management side can explain much of the restricted diffusion at the national level.

The discussions and debates preceding the new corporate assembly legislation in 1972 form another strong factor which diverted management and union interest away from the Cooperation Project. Now the uncertainties about the operation of this new law are removed, management might be more interested in developing initiatives in this area.

Finally the job design principles as presented by the Norwegian researchers are somewhat unconventional and notions like a 'continuous learning process' and 'autonomous work group' are sometimes difficult to understand and grasp in practical terms for many people. This lack of understanding creates ambiguity which hinders the diffusion process. This 'ambiguity' is particularly evident in Norwegian trade union circles.

Intra-company Diffusion. If management and unions have decided to start work in this area what are the problems they are faced with which constrain changing the work organization and in a latter phase interfere with the spreading of some of the changes to other departments within the company? A number of factors will be listed here, others will be presented in the discussion of the union role which follows. Factors which constrain implementation and spreading of new forms of work organization within a company:

1. Lacking top management and/or union support. This support is not only necessary to legitimize the changes in work organization but also to acquire necessary organizational back up. Field reports often cite lack of top management support as a cause of stagnation. Agreement to start a change process is not sufficient, active management and union involvement and support is necessary in a job redesign process.

2. Inadequate resources. Time, money, technical and social know-how of change processes, and organizational 'room' to maneuver are logical requirements. Lack of technical and social know-how inside the organization leads to a situation where the project development becomes completely dependent on the outside researchers. In the early phases, transfer of skills to people active in the change process is necessary in order to assure continuation after the researchers withdraw. The workers involved should have time and other resources to get active in the process of changing their jobs. Creation of 'free space' (Herbst, 1974) to enable maneuvering in an experiment is necessary. Some 'free space' is always present in the

formal organizational structure but it can be increased by generally reducing the specifications and prescriptions for worker behavior.

3. Supervisors and lower management often feel threatened by a project. If no provisions are made for changes in the role and functions of these groups they could stop the change process. This requires that the unit of change becomes much larger than the original work group. Stagnation will always result if the larger organization does not change. This is in accordance with systems theory which states that it is unlikely that changes in a part will be sustained over time if the changes are not reciprocated by sufficient adjustments in the total system. Job redesign underlines these interdependencies within an organization.

4. Technological barriers. Not only the larger organization but also technology puts severe constraints on the possibilities for change. Process technology seems particularly suitable for increasing autonomy and learning. Assembly technology also is rather suited to the introduction of e.g. autonomous work groups. Other technologies seem to present more serious difficulties.

5. Bad physical conditions. Gulowsen et al. (1973*) found that experiments were more successful in companies with good physical working conditions. These conditions probably reflect both a management attitude and certain technological aspects. Bad physical conditions were correlated with negative experimental results.

6. Inadequate worker skills. In their study Gulowsen et al. (1973*) also found that experiments were more successful with skilled workers than with unskilled workers. The first group is probably more responsive to increased autonomy and learning in their jobs.

7. The promotion of prime movers in a project. In most social change programs dynamic persons are required to activate a process of change. In the case of successful projects these 'key' individuals are very often promoted. Managers move up in the company hierarchy and union representatives in either the company or union hierarchy. Through this departure of key personnel the experimental department loses both leadership and skills. The change process as a result often loses its momentum.

8. Union and worker resistance. These problems will be discussed in the following part of this chapter.

Trade unions in most developed countries are confronted with difficulties in establishing policies and activities in the area of job redesign. Even in Norway and Sweden where policy statements of the national federations of trade unions clearly endorse job design as a method to increase workers' autonomy and improve working conditions at the shop floor level, the same federations have great problems in making these issues lively ones within their own organizations. The U.S. unions seem very hesitant in endorsing job redesign as a method to improve job satisfaction of the individual worker (e.g. Brooks, 1972; Winpisinger, 1973). In Germany and the Netherlands the unions have not taken a position yet and in France the unions are divided on the issue. Only in Italy have trade unions succeeded to include demands for job enlargement in their agreements with Fiat and Olivetti. The unions however do not participate in the job redesign process and the clauses regarding job enlargement come very close to upgrading clauses in U.S. contracts. The main differences are the method by which this upgrading is achieved and the important fact that some undesirable jobs are eliminated. In addition to the possible danger that management can use job redesign in a unilateral manner to increase productivity there are at least five fundamental problems which make it difficult for unions to incorporate job redesign in their major operating policies:

1. the underlying individual ethic of job redesign is directly opposed to the union's collective ethic.
2. the specifics of job redesign are very difficult to incorporate in a collective bargaining agreement.
3. there are no clear demands from the shop floor for job redesign.
4. job redesign can upset the existing system of job regulation as developed by unions.
5. the bureaucratic rigidities of the unions' organizational structures.

Historically labor unions have found their 'raison d'etre' in protecting the collective interests of their members. The essence of this collective ethic was early acknowledged by the Webbs:

'In unorganized trades the individual workman, applying for a job, accepts or refuses the terms offered by the employer without communication with his fellow-workmen, and without any other consideration than the exigencies of his own position. For the sale of his labor he makes, with the employer, a strictly individual bargain. But if a group of workmen concert together, and send representatives to conduct the bargaining on behalf of the whole body, the position is at once changed. Instead of the employer making a series of separate contracts with isolated individuals, he meets with a collective will, and settles, in a single agreement, *the principles upon which, for the time being, all workmen of a particular group, or class, or grade, will engaged'*.   (Webb and Webb, 1902, 178).[14]

14. Emphasis added.

The central goal of unionism has been the furthering of the collective worker interests through enforcement of the 'common rules'. The logic of unionism is to further the interest of the individual worker by improving the conditions for the collectivity. The emphasis is clearly on the latter. The individual interest is secured through collective effort and collective regulation. For the large majority of industrial workers the historical choice in favor for collective advancement was a rational one. Organizational conditions and structures of the large industrial enterprises offer only very limited chances for individual advancement in the form of a career. Collective advancement through unionization has been the method chosen by large groups of workers in the industrialized countries. The collective ethic is probably even stronger in those countries where the unions have close ties to the social-democratic political parties. The ethic underlying job redesign is in its logic exactly opposed to the union ethic. Job design programs are highly individualistic and situational in their orientation, the emphasis is on the individual job, on individual satisfaction, in individual learning, and on individual motivation. The underlying logic is that by changing the job of the individual worker the collective interest of all workers will be furthered. This reversal of individual and collectivity can explain some of the difficulties unions have in relating to the job design ideas as described in Chapter 3.

Unions have not paid primary attention to the problems of the individual in his immediate task. The craft-unions did not develop their system of job regulation and job control to provide the worker a more interesting job. The primary motivation was to protect the collectivity, in this case the craft, against competition from 'less skilled' workers. In the U.S. a local union represents and bargains on behalf of *all* workers in a bargaining unit. This service to the collectivity is also clear in the U.S. grievance procedure where individual grievances are taken up but the union local takes due account of the interest of *all* workers in processing grievances. Woodcock describes the impact of the grievance procedure on the collectivity as follows 'every grievance launched into the procedure will have the ripple effect of a smaller or larger stone thrown into a pool' (Woodcock, 1974, 204). Job classification, work assignment, and seniority disputes are much more than individual complaints. They have direct importance for the relative standing of different groups of workers and determine their perception of equity. These examples are given to underline the collectivistic nature of union behavior. The individual nature of job redesign is hard to fit into the unions' institutional framework which is geared at dealing with collectivities. Job redesign requires an individual orientation.

Recent developments in Norway seem to support this argument. The problems of the internal industrial environment and safety and health issues have become very important within the trade unions. LO has appointed a special secretary to deal with these issues and the national unions are very active. This is sharp contrast to their behavior in the field of job redesign. The difference in union behavior can in my opinion partly be explained by the collective nature of the health and safety issues. The health and safety issues fit the institutional framework of dealing with collectivist problems, legislations can be passed and collective bargaining agreements can be adapted. Job redesign just does not fit the collectivist ethic of unionism and for this reason has yet to become routinized into union's institutional machinery. The problem of fitting job redesign as a major issue into day-to-day union policy is probably more severe at the national level than at the local level. The Norwegian experiments have demonstrated that local unions can become very active in this area but innovative and strong local leadership seem to be a necessary prerequisite.

Directly connected with the issue of the collective ethic is the problem of incorporating anything more than general job design principles into a collective bargaining agreement. Providing for detailed regulation in this area is impossible, and even undesirable. The actual process of redesigning a job cannot be handled in a collective bargaining setting. Collective bargaining is crucial however in: 1. creating the necessary safeguards and guarantees to the workers before the start of a job design project; and 2. adapting the wage levels and wage systems to the new conditions of work. The safeguards and guarantees for the workers are usually laid down in a so-called shelter agreement.[15]

This agreement generally includes clauses which settle the manning levels, define the experimental area, regulate the wage development, provide for voluntary participation of the workers, and give both management and the union the right to stop the experiment whenever they desire to do so. Following the job redesign process the issues of upgrading, sharing the increased productivity, and dealing with changes in the work effort bargain are clearly issues which have to be referred back to the regular collective bargaining process. Negotiations have to be at a very decentralized level in order for a union to adequately deal with these issues. The bargaining process can provide the context for a job design experiment and in a later phase deal with the results of the change process. The job design process itself can only be

15. Appendix 1 contains two examples of such shelter agreements: one of a Norwegian company, the other of a U.S. firm which generally follows the Thorsrud approach.

handled outside the bargaining procedure by the workers immediately involved in close cooperation with management and union representatives.

The third general problem facing unions in this area is the lack of strong demands for job redesign from the shop floor. As pointed out before, job redesign proposals initially receive a very cool reception by the workers involved. The Norwegian experiments show that *only experience* with the new forms of work organization seem to generate positive worker attitudes. It is very difficult for people to demand and evaluate conditions of work they have never experienced. Fox (1971, 13) also emphasizes the importance of experience 'in order to make a rational choice as between the full range of intrinsic and extrinsic rewards one must have experienced both sorts in all that they have to offer, and this condition is not fulfilled for major proportions of industrial populations'.

A LO representative summarized the attitudes of the workers in the first four demonstration companies as follows: 'Our members were very much satisfied. They had got the opportunity to learn more about their own jobs, to be trained to do more than one job and to take part in decision-making in the department. The wage system was changed from single piece rate to basic wages combined with a bonus system . . . the best evidence of member satisfaction is the fact that nobody wants to go back to the old system' (Larsen, 1974, 3 and 5). The empirical support for the 'experience hypothesis' in the Norwegian experiments makes a stimulating union role at the local level very important.

The picture of worker satisfaction after job design changes is complicated, as evidenced by the quotes from Fox and Larsen, by the fact that these changes are very often combined with the introduction of a fixed wage system and with wage increases through upgrading or higher productivity. It is of course very difficult to isolate the increased job satisfaction. Experiments at Philips in the Netherlands however indicate that positive worker attitudes are also the result of changes in job design without any increases in wages. The central work council of Philips has demanded expansion of the 'job structuring' projects despite the fact that at Philips no wage increases resulted from the changes in work organization (Philips, 1973*). The fact remains however that only in a very few cases workers demand changes in their work organization. Lack of experience with different organizational forms contributes to the lack of demands in this area.

The fourth problem is the relationship between job regulation and job redesign. It is certainly no surprise that the Norwegian Graphical Union is very much against job redesign as proposed in the Norwegian Cooperation

Project. Graphical unions are classical examples of craft unions which through their regulation virtually control the shop floor in the printing trades. The union promotion system and job definitions regulate the work organization. It certainly does not provide for a very flexible system but the printers have been able to maintain their craft in face of fast technological developments (see also Barbash (1974b) on this issue). The printers have refused cooperation in one company. In another Norwegian printing firm a Cooperation Project has been started but this project is centered around the introduction of a council system which provides for better labor-management communications. No changes have been made in the work organization itself. Workers have developed vested interests in the system of job regulation, in many cases specialization has been halted through this formal craft control. It is therefore quite understandable that we can expect resistance in the craft unions against job redesign.

Finally the unions in Norway suffer from the same organizational regidities as industrial organizations. The highly centralized structures of LO and its national unions do not leave ample room for initiative and innovation at the lower levels of these organizations. Trade unions are exposed to the same societal changes as industrial organizations; the unions' response in terms of organizational adaptation has been negligible so far. Also *within* unions there is a need for job redesign as a method to increase organizational flexibility by reducing excessive bureaucratic regulations.

Changing the emphasis to a more practical level, which major problems does the local union face in participating in a job design project? Let us assume that management and unions have decided to start working in the area of job redesign, a shelter agreement has been signed, and changes in the work organization have been successfully implemented. In other words the experiment has been a success within the experimental area. Workers in this area have attained better working conditions, more interesting work and little higher wages. The question of how to transfer the conditions of the experimental area to the rest of the organization becomes crucial.

In practice it does not seem possible to maintain differential working conditions over any extended period of time. Very soon the workers in the non-experimental areas demand the same conditions and in many cases it has not been possible to extend the new conditions to the other departments. The union is faced with worker demands from other departments for equity. Trondhjem Mek-Verksted is an example of a company where a rather successful experiment had to be stopped because the union was unable to obtain the same conditions for all its members. This comparison process seems to be very important and has played a significant role in many experiments. The experimental area can only be sheltered for a certain period of time, about one or at the most two years, hereafter equity pressures are building up very quickly. The individual changes in job design are impossible to transfer to other departments. Different solutions are most likely required in these departments and this change process takes time.

At Norsk Hydro and some other companies some of these problems were avoided by implementing the new wage system and training opportunities of the experimental plants into the collective agreement covering all Norsk Hydro plants. The individual changes in job design cannot be transferred in a similar fashion however. Management and unions have to be aware of this problem before starting an experiment. The only practical solution is that larger parts of the organization become involved in the change process. Isolated changes in one particular area do not have much chance to survive in an organization operating under different principles; in addition workers will demand equitable and fair treatment after some period of time. In practice it seems that the comparison process by which workers evaluate the fairness of their position seems to work faster than the process of organizational change.

A critical decision has to be made at this point and in several instances the possibility of speeding up the diffusion process was rejected. The predominant response seems to be to stop the change process in the experimental area and to refer back to the previous work situation. This raises the question of the power relationships in an experiment. The shelter agreement usually provides that the experiment is continued only if both parties (management and union) desire to do so. This gives the union and management the power to stop an experiment if it is evaluated negatively from their respective points of view. The workers and their union do not have the power to continue an experiment they consider successful, but which is evaluated negatively by management. Management does not always seem to realize the consequences of an experiment. Skard of the NAF warns his members 'that management should realize before they commit themselves to experimentation that this kind of experiment is quite different in its effect from for instance trying out a new machine or new technique' (Skard, 1973, 7). Workers can become activated through the change process and demand further changes which touch upon the lower and middle management levels. In such instances the managerial prerogative still prevails and the experiment will most likely be stopped.

The interrelationship between job design and the wage system has already been mentioned before. In all Norwegian experiments the wage system has become a central issue in the change process. It seems to support those observers (e.g. Barbash, 1971, Daniel and McIntosh, 1972) who argue that 'the price of labor is inseparable from the manner in which it is to be utilized. It is all part of the effort bargain' (Barbash, 1971, Ch. 5, 1). Changing the conditions of work which sometimes includes the reduction of manning, necessarily implies not only changes in wage system but also in the wage rate. The active union role in the Norwegian experiments has assured that these issues plus the possible increases in productivity will be transferred very quickly to the bargaining table.

The general experience in Norway has been that participation in a job design experiment has a favorable impact upon the degree of unionization within the companies. At Hunsfos and Norsk Hydro the active union role led to an increase in union membership. In both cases almost 100% of the work force became organized.

In the successful demonstration companies (Norsk Hydro, Hunsfos) the local union has been very active with a result that the scope of bargaining has been considerably extended, in particular in the areas of learning on the job, training, and education. The role of the union in the new wave of 14 experimental companies (see Table 9, p. 53) is on the whole considerably less active. In most cases the union takes a wait and see attitude instead of an active role. The reasons for this more passive attitude have been partly discussed above, in addition we can say that management in these 14 companies has even a much stronger problem orientation than in the earlier experiments. Under these conditions the union falls back in its traditional reactive role and will only become involved if the members' interests are perceived to be threatened.

Before presenting the final conclusions of this chapter two more theoretical aspects of organizational change processes will be discussed: the character of organizational change and the relationship between the organization and its environment.

Although the 'continuous learning process' is a key concept in the work of the AFI researchers (e.g. Thorsrud and Emery, 1970*) the Norwegian job redesign experiments show with almost no exception the occurrence of a stagnation phase in the change process. Other European experiments support the generality of such a stagnation phase (Van der Does, 1973). Stagnation means in some instances the definite end of the change process, in other experiments the stagnation has a more temporary character. As indicated earlier in this chapter the causes of limited diffusion and stagnation are both of an organizational system and an individual-personal nature. The latter obstacle led the AFI researchers to emphasize education in organizational change programs.

A continuous learning and organizational change process must therefore be understood as a stepwise instead of linear process. The general change process in the Norwegian experiments is realistically depicted by the change model presented in the sociological literature. Hage and Aiken (1970) in their model of organizational change put great emphasis on a routinization stage in the change process. In this stage the organization attempts to stabilize the effects of the changes. The changes become standardized for the larger organization.

In the experiments with Norsk Hydro and Hunsfos the incorporation of some of the changes in the research sites into the collective bargaining agreement can be seen as such organizational routinization. After the routinization no immediate new changes were initiated. The new equilibrium will probably remain until management or the union recognizes, or is forced to recognize, the need for new changes. This routinization stage explains fairly well the stagnation in many experiments. Failure to routinize the changes often means the end of the experimental conditions in the research sites. The time period between different phases of change can vary, but the Norwegian experiments suggest them to be rather long. In the Hunsfos case the time period between the different phases was about two years.

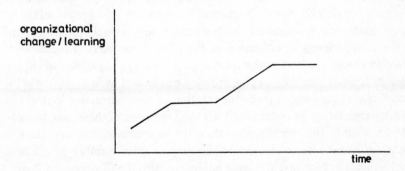

Figure 1. The step-wise model of organizational change.

The Norwegian experiments also provide some support for the environment-organization hypothesis, but in a somewhat different form than suggested by Emery and Trist (1965). The impact of the environment on the organization is postulated following open systems theory which states that an organization has to adapt itself to its changing environment in order to survive. The increasing turbulence in the environment requires a more flexible organizational structure which can be provided by the implementation of the job design principles as described in Chapter 3. These new forms of work organization will create the necessary organizational flexibility (O.E.C.D., 1974(b)).

Emery and Trist (1965) define the relevant organizational environment predominantly in terms of other *organizations* (competitors in the product market and government in its regulative role). Gulowsen et al. (1973*) conclude that the companies which have participated in the experiments so far did not face a more turbulent environment than other Norwegian companies in terms of their market and government environment. In most instances the experimental companies manufactured products with a very long life cycle. Gulowsen et al. (1973*, 65) summarize this part of their evaluation as follows: 'Our analysis does not provide us with a basis to answer the question whether a cooperation project can represent a strategy for adaptation to a turbulent environment at a national level'.

The recent wave of new experiments in Norway is a clear response to the labor market.[16] This particular segment of the organizational environment differs from Emery and Trist's (1965) conceptualization of the environment in terms of other *organizations*. Changes in the labor market are reflected in new behavior patterns of the *individuals* making up the relevant labor supply for a company. The Norwegian labor market has in the last couple of years changed in both quantitative and qualitative aspects. It has become more stringent, particularly in certain regional areas, through the growth of the oil related industries. Changes in the Norwegian educational system and the higher average levels of education of the labor force make it increasingly difficult to recruit labor for unattractive positions. The expansion of the job redesign projects into the shipping industry was caused by innovations in the educational system which made the creation of more attractive jobs in this industry mandatory in order to attract the graduates of these new schools.

In addition to the experiments within the individual companies, the Cooperation Project has had considerable impact on a number of national developments in Norway. The wide publicity which the Cooperation Project received in the national press and in large numbers of seminars had the following effects at a national level:

16. The changes in the labor market have led to an increased convergence between the Norwegian and Swedish experiments in this area.

1. An increased awareness among workers and management about possible alternative forms of work organization.
2. Time and motion studies (MTM) are definitely on their way out in Norway. The experiments also stimulated changes in the area of wage systems. Piece rates seem to be generally replaced by a fixed wage system with maximal 20% bonus. Larsen (LO secretary) gave this evaluation of the impact of the experiments: 'The situation today is that piece rates, time study and MTM system are on the way out, and we are glad for this development' (Larsen, 1974, 4).
3. A strong emphasis on the relationship between work and education. The need for recurrent education and training at the company level are becoming important issues in Norway today.

These changes are also taking place in other West-European countries. In Norway however the Cooperation Project seems to have played an important catalyzing role.

Despite the limited diffusion that has taken place in Norway and the few companies in which substantial changes have been achieved, the Cooperation Project has proved that changes in work organization which increase worker autonomy are possible under certain conditions without hampering productivity and efficiency. Gulowsen et al. (1973*, 2) see the main contribution of the Cooperation Project as 'Norwegian workers have showed themselves fully competent to manage themselves and their daily work both in production and service sectors'. This is an important conclusion despite that 'manage themselves' must be seen in the context of a larger organizational structure which both constrains and facilitates the development of an individual's autonomy at work. A few cases highlighted that initial worker resistance and a number of organizational constraints can be overcome in a change process with as one of its outcomes increased skill levels and autonomy for the workers. This chapter also attempted to enumerate the factors which impeded a fast spreading process of the new job design principles in Norway. The embeddedness of the work group in a larger company organized on different principles seems to be the primary obstacle in an intra-company spreading and change process. The Cooperation Project also showed that through job redesign experiments both management and unions can reach some of their traditional objectives. The new forms of work organization do have a positive impact on efficiency and productivity while the union can obtain somewhat higher wages and upgrading opportunities for their members. In addition to these traditional objectives worker autonomy in the immediate task can be increased.

The Norwegian experiments show that job redesign indeed can be treated as an issue of an integrative nature in labor-management relations. The fact that most experiments are initiated by management is by some union people not seen as a disadvantage. Ryste states: 'In the case of management initiative you know that management wants to move. There is a certain commitment to do something in this area. This makes the union position considerably less ambivalent' (Ryste, interview, 1974). The next chapter will evaluate to what extent these type of experiments contribute to industrial democracy, which was the original aim of the Norwegian Cooperation Project. The new wave of recent experiments clearly has much more limited objectives. Thorsrud's job design principles are still very much alive in Norway today. The following paragraph from the 1974 LO-NAF Basic Agreement underlines the willingness of the social partners to continue their support for projects in this area.

'It is important that in each company an effort is made to find forms of cooperation which, given its own special circumstances, can realize the cooperation goals[17] as formulated in this agreement. As a start in this direction LO and NAF agree to support further research and development with as goal to find forms of work organization and cooperation which provide all employees with increasing opportunities to participate in the redesign of his work and work place – see e.g. the research carried out under the Cooperation project LO-NAF. The local partners should therefore look for areas within their company where research can be carried out'.

(LO-NAF, 1974*, 38).

17. In the first draft of this new paragraph the main referent was democratic developments inside the undertaking. Under pressure from NAF this paragraph was redrafted in co-operation terminology.

5. Job redesign one element in the ,,package approach'' towards industrial democracy

OVERVIEW
Approaches towards industrial democracy – underlying model of man – representative versus participatory democracy – some history – definition of industrial democracy – approaches used in Norway – the package approach – limitations – public interest – conclusions.

Industrial democracy is one of the more overworked concepts in parts of the social science literature and in the writings of political activists. Recently industrial democracy has been mentioned in connection with factory occupations by protesting workers (e.g. The French Lip and Dutch Enka affaires), union behavior and collective bargaining (Clegg, 1960; Derber, 1969), the discussions about a new Common Market company law in Brussels (Blanpain, 1974), codetermination in Germany (Wilpert, 1973), the Yugoslav model of workers' self management (Broekmeyer, 1969; Adizes, 1971), workers' control (Gorz, 1968; Hunnius et al., 1973), job design and autonomous work groups (Emery and Thorsrud, 1969; Blumberg, 1968). Underlying all these is a common value perspective which accepts that in the modern enterprises the interests of workers are not adequately represented in the organizational decision making processes. All the approaches listed above attempt to create a better representation of the worker interest in the organizational decision making process.[1]

The organizational model used in the discussions of industrial democracy differs considerably from the monolithic organizational model found in the classical management and human relations schools. Within organizations the existence of a number of groups with different interests, goals, and values is taken for granted. The members of an organization possess a variety of interests which they seek to advance and protect in their association with it,

1. For the Webbs (1902) and many others industrial democracy goes far beyond the enterprise level. Industrial democracy for them was a society in which industry would be run by the workers under a charter negotiated with government, that would protect the interests of the community. In much of the discussion that follows industrial democracy is used in the much narrower sense of organizational democracy. The term industrial democracy is maintained because: 1. the Norwegian Cooperation Project was particularly in its beginning strongly linked to the industrial democracy debate in Norway; and 2. much of the literature (wrongly) uses industrial democracy in the sense of organizational democracy.

and these interests may harmonize or conflict with each other in varying degrees (see e.g. Fox, 1971). A model of man is accepted, either implicitly of explicitly, which suggests that individuals make decisions to some extent on the basis of their self-interest. Therefore, the greater the distance of an organizational member from where a decision is made, the less his own interests are likely to be compatible with that decision (Weick, 1969). The different approaches towards industrial democracy are all attempts to assure that workers as much as possible shall be able to influence those decisions which are of concern to them. A basic distinction can be made between indirect or representative methods to achieve industrial democracy and direct or participatory approaches. An example of the former is the collective bargaining process while the Norwegian job redesign experiments represent the participatory approach.

A clear dichotomy exists in the literature between those who advocate participatory democracy and those who reject the particpatory model mainly on practical grounds. In the political sphere, contemporary theorizing pays only minimal attention to the issue of active participaton. The dominant empirical perspective tends to restricts democracy to a political method with its dominant dimension being the formal voting procedure for electing political leaders.[2] Lindsay (1962, 25) states the basic postulate of this school 'The people cannot govern but they may control'. Control, of course, is exercised through the election of representatives. Clegg (1960) takes a position somewhat similar to this representative model of political democracy as he defines industrial democracy in terms of management and unions, the representatives of the workers, as countervailing forces. Participation of the workers beyond union representation will jeopardize both the power and the independence of the union: in other words Clegg perceives participation beyond the indirect form as a threat to industrial democracy. This collective bargaining approach towards industrial democracy represents fairly well the position of most trade unions in the Anglo-Saxon countries. Sturmthal (1969, 150) evaluates the U.S. developments as follows: 'A study of industrial democracy in the U.S. in this century is thus almost exclusively an examination of the extent to and the way in which collective bargaining has been used as an instrument to bring about a measure of industrial democracy'.

In sharp contrast to the representative school we find the participatory democracy theorists (e.g. G. D. H. Cole, J. S. Mill). They generally share a strong belief in environmental determinism. Changing the existing authority

2. See Pateman (1970) for a discussion of the representative versus the participatory schools in political theory.

patterns and increasing the participation of the individual in public and company affairs will contribute to the widening of the individual's horizons. The major function of increased participation as perceived by these thinkers is in fact an educative one. In the industrial sphere many theorists have advocated over time the idea that workers should exert some form of control over the process of production.[3]

In the early nineteenth century Fourier, and at a more practical level Owen, suggested a return to small artisan communities as an answer to the increasing degradation of man caused by the industrial revolution. These utopian ideas of a return to a decentralized small scale society influenced the later anarchists like Kropotkin and Bakunin. They not only saw the workers' seizure of power at the local level as an attempt to improve the conditions at work, but also as a necessary protection against the coercive nature of the state. Marx himself, in his early work, deplored the alienated condition of the industrial worker in the capitalist society but saw the transfer in the ownership of production as the only way to change this situation. The end result would be the not very well developed 'free association of producers'. In the early part of this century the British guild socialists (in particular G. D. H. Cole) set forth their ideas about a participatory industrial society. The spirit of community and solidarity should be recreated by organizing each industry into a guild. These guilds would include *all* workers in an industry. The guilds were proposed to be completely autonomous in dealing with their internal affairs. The guild socialists honestly believed that 'almost no regulation would be necessary as the instincts of pride, honor, and workmanship would reassert themselves under the guild system' (Wachtel, 1973, 23-25). The syndicalists aimed at the same goals as the guild socialists: industrial democracy and the abolition of the state. Instead of peaceful change through encroaching control by collective bargaining, the syndicalists advocated the general strike and industrial agitation as the means by which trade unions would assume control over the economy. More recently the 'New Left' has incorporated many of the above ideas in their proposals. In Western Europe the New Left seems to be predominantly Maoist or anarchist. All these intellectual streams of thought have had influence on the earlier listed approaches to increase industrial democracy, in particular on those that provide for a direct participatory system of democracy.

Emery and Thorsrud (1969) and also Blumberg (1968), relying on a social psychological model of individual growth, also advocate increased participa-

3. The historical discussion that follows is based upon Gide and Rist (1909) and Wachtel (1973, Ch. 5).

tion of the worker, but initially only in a restricted area: the immediate job. For Emery and Thorsrud changes attained in the individiual job through job redesign do not represent industrial democracy in themselves, but they see the improvements in the conditions for personal participation in the immediate job area as a *necessary* condition for any real worker participation in management. The experimental changes in their view do not represent industrial democracy but only set the stage for a possible take-off in that direction.

This tie to industrial democracy is a little uneasy. This uneasiness is basically caused by the fact that in contrast to most writers on industrial democracy Emery and Thorsrud do not work with a conflict model of organizations. Thorsrud in Norway has depoliticized the notion of industrial democracy by focusing at technology and the organizational control system as the main factors obstructing a change to a more democratic organization. The premise of this approach is that both management and workers have common interests with regard to changing the organizational structure. It is this premise which makes it difficult to fit the Thorsrud approach into the more classical approaches towards participatory democracy. Thorsrud does not deny the existence of conflicting interests within organizations and the necessity of trade unions, but he perceives the changes in job redesign as an issue of an integrative nature. It is the purpose of this chapter to describe and analyze the several approaches which in Norway are used to increase industrial democracy and evaluate the Cooperation Project in this context. My general thesis is that the different approaches towards industrial democracy serve different functions and are by no means mutually exclusive. In the words of Walker (1970, 34) 'More progress would be made towards industrial democracy if it were recognized that we cannot expect any form of industrial democracy to perform the functions of others'. The 'Package Approach' can be defined as the simultaneous use of different approaches to attain industrial democracy.

Two caveats are in order here. First the analogy between political and industrial democracy is not a perfect one. Democracy, in the political sphere, is associated with government by the people, or rule by those being ruled, through elected representatives. Transferring this idea of democracy to the industrial sphere one has to imagine an industrial firm wherein the employees by majority vote, elect the board of the company, its managing director and other important officers, and determine business policy. The goal of the industrial firm differs however from the goal of a democratic political system. The overriding goal of an industrial firm is production and not the protection of the employees' interests; this in contrast to the general aim of a democratic political system. One should also note that participation and democracy are not synonyms. 'Not only is it possible for partial participation at both management levels to take place without a democratization of authority structures, but it is also possible for full participation to be introduced at a lower level within the context of a non-democratic authority structure overall' (Pateman, 1970, 73). Given the explicit production goals of our industrial system and its concomittant industrial tensions (Barbash, 1972) the conceptualization of democracy and participation in a relative manner is a more fruitful approach from an analytic point of view.

From viewing industrial democracy in a relative manner to a conceptualization of industrial democracy as a variable is the final step in an effort to analyze more precisely the different approaches towards industrial democracy. This conceptualization makes the following definition of industrial democracy possible: industrial democracy is the extent to which workers and their representatives influence the outcome or organizational decisions.[4] Two elements are central to this definition. The workers' ability to influence and the organizational decisions. The former can be labeled the workers' relative strength and the latter the domain of industrial democracy. The workers' strength is the degree or probability that workers or their representatives can determine the outcome of a certain organizational decision making process. This strength is a relational concept. It is not the absolute strength, but the relative strength compared to management which decides the outcome of a decision making process. The domain of industrial democracy refers to the number of organizational decisions over which the workers or their representatives can exercise some influence. It is of course not only the sheer number which determines the degree of industrial democracy but also the importance of the decisions from the workers' point of view. In other words the weight the workers or their union attach to a certain decision. The argument can be functionally represented as:

Industrial democracy $= f (D \times W \times S)$

$D =$ domain (the number of decisions)
$W =$ weight (the importance of each decision to the workers)
$S =$ strength (probability that workers can determine each decisional outcome)

4. Participation can now be defined as the presence of workers or their representatives during a decision making process without substantially influencing the decision outcome.

From this it follows that an organization is more democratic when the workers or their representatives have a greater probability to determine the outcome of a large number of important organizational decisions than an organization where the probability is low that they determine a small number of not so important decisions. Several other combinations are of course possible. This conceptualization of industrial democracy is clearly an over-simplification, but it allows for a more concrete analysis of different approaches towards industrial democracy.

Decisions which are of direct importance to the workers are made at several levels within an organization and also in places beyond the individual company. The following levels of decision making can be distinguished:

1. national   3. company   5. department   7. individual job
2. industry   4. plant   6. work group

The direct form of participatory democracy is generally restricted to the individual job and work group level. Elected representatives look after the workers' interests at the higher organizational and supra-organizational levels.

The Norwegian industrial relations system has developed the following forms or approaches whereby the workers or their representatives can have varying degrees of influence over decision making outcomes at the different levels of the system:

national	1	– legislation
	2	collective bargaining LO/NAF
industry		– collective bargaining
company	3	– board representation
	4	corporate assembly
		collective bargaining
plant	5	– work council
		collective bargaining
	6	shop steward system
	7	safety and health shop steward
department	8	– department council
		shop steward system
work group	9	– work and job regulation democratization
		shop steward system
individual job	10	– work democratization
		shop steward system

These forms to increase industrial democracy will be briefly discussed and summarized in terms of the earlier presented functional form of industrial democracy.

Legislation

A strong position of DNA in the Norwegian legislature gives the labor movement the opportunity to influence many important decisions at a national level. Issues like unemployment benefits, health insurance, pension schemes, safety and health regulations, which in the U.S. are taken up in the collective bargaining process, are settled at a national level and cover *all* workers. Legislation also introduced the worker representation on the company boards of directors and the corporate assembly.[5] This approach to attain industrial democracy is only briefly mentioned here because of its rather limited direct impact on the democratization of undertakings.

Table 11. Legislation.

domain	:	unemployment benefits, health insurance, pension schemes, social security, safety and health regulations etc.
weight	:	important, particularly from a social class and worker collectivity point of view.
strength	:	strong ability to determine decision making outcomes if pro-labor parties have majority in legislature.

Collective bargaining

This method of increasing industrial democracy still is the most powerful in both the U.S. and the West-European countries. Collective bargaining is both a way of introducing industrial democracy and industrial democracy in itself. It is a process of decision making with as its overriding purpose 'the negotiation of an agreed set of rules to govern the substantive and procedural terms of the employment relationship, as well as the relationship between the bargaining parties themselves' (ILO, 1974, 7). Collective bargaining is a form of representative democracy, but the bargaining process can take place

5. See Chapter 2, pp. 29-30.

at different levels of the industrial relations system: ranging from plant level bargaining to the bargaining at the national level. The potential use of the strike puts the representatives of the workers on fairly equal terms with the management representatives in the collective bargaining process. In Barbash's (1974, 29) words 'bargaining is based on the workers' own collective power to withhold their labor. Only the bargaining type of transaction rests on this measure of equality among the parties.' Some observers (Clegg, 1960; Derber, 1969) equate collective bargaining with industrial democracy. This view implies that 'workers can only participate in management from the outside, by pressure, and normally through representatives' (Clegg, 1960, 132). In this view participation becomes somewhat a contradiction in terms.

The bargaining process is a give and take between the parties which results in the collective bargaining agreement. This agreement is binding upon management. It provides the workers and their union a number of rights which, if necessary, can be defended in the courts of law. The first line of defense against management breaking the terms of the agreement in the U.S. is the grievance procedure in which unions can take up possible management violations of workers' rights as established in the agreement. Bargaining on subjects like wages, working time, job classification, and grievances means that the employers do not decide alone on these matters and that those decisions are the result of negotiation between the employer and the trade union. The scope of bargaining, the number of issues that are brought up in the negotiations, differs from country to country. In the U.S. the bargaining scope is probably the widest. Issues like health schemes, pensions, unemployment benefits, which in Norway are provided for by legislation, are an important part of collective bargaining in the U.S. Also issues which in Norway are settled in the plant and department councils, like protective clothing, scheduling of vacation, and quality of coffee in the canteens, are subject to bargaining in the U.S. In Norway the bargaining at the industry level is basically focused around wage issues and job classification schemes, local agreements have the functions of applying the terms of the contract to the specific company conditions. Bargaining is indeed the most powerful method of advancing the worker interests, however it is clear that the union power can only be applied to a small number of demands in each bargaining session. The number of issues that can be dealt with is also restricted. Therefore other forms to attain industrial democracy could well supplement collective bargaining.

Table 12. Collective bargaining.

domain	:	Wages and working conditions. Scope of bargaining in Norway smaller than in U.S.
weight	:	Very important. Wages and working conditions are the raison d'etre of unionism. Issues brought into the bargaining process are ideally articulated in the union structure based upon shop floor desires.
strength	:	The use of the strike threat provides the union with a powerful position which can be exploited with respect to certain demands.

Board representation[6]

This form of representation of the workers' interest in organizational decision making was first introduced in Germany after the Second World War. In the thirty years since, several European countries have adopted similar schemes which generally provide for a minority representation of workers on the board of directors. Such schemes are currently practiced in Germany, Austria, Norway, Sweden, and Denmark. This list of countries will increase substantially if the Common Market Company bills become finally enacted upon. The minority representation of the workers assures that they do not have decisive influence over decision making outcomes of the board. So far only the codetermination scheme in the German coal and steel industry provides for parity representation.

Gustavsen (1972*) studied the board of directors of the approximately 200 largest companies in Norway. He described the general function of the board as that of embedding the organization in a larger societal framework. The board of directors was important in linking the company to financial institutions, local and national government, and to other companies. The predominant orientation of the board was of an outward looking nature. Practical company decision making did not take place in board meetings. The minority representation of workers on the board and the nature of the issues discussed does not make this form of representation a very lively one among the shop floor workers.

6. This is a general discussion of board representation. Technical differences between one and two-tier structure and the Dutch alternative to board representation are not included here.

Fürstenberg reported surveys of German workers which have shown that, while most of them know that codetermination took place in their under- taking, only half had any definite idea as to its purpose and only one in ten 'had some knowledge of the actual composition of the supervisory board' (Fürstenberg, 1969, 130). Fürstenberg's study generally supports Emery and Thorsrud's (1969)[7] argument about the lack of any significant impact of board representation on the shop floor. Emery and Thorsrud stressed in particular the tendency among worker representatives to conform to the behavior of the regular board members. This socialization process could easily create an estrangement from the shop floor constituency.

Within the presented 'package approach' towards industrial democracy it must be questioned to what extent 'impact on the shop floor' is the correct evaluation criterion of board representation. From a larger industrial demo- cracy perspective board representation provides worker representatives with a considerable amount of new information, which was previously secret, that can be used e.g. in collective bargaining. Also after introduction of worker representation social issues seem to play a more important role in board meetings (Blume, 1962*; Fürstenberg, 1969; Wilpert, 1973). In addition, the mere fact of worker representation could have a certain 'preventive impact'.

The direct influence of the worker representatives on the decision out- comes seems to be very limited. Blume (1962*) concludes that the partity representation in the coal and steel industry in Germany exerts no influence whatever in the economic field. It may be said that codetermination in Germany has so far had effects on social policy but not on economic policy (Fürstenberg, 1969). These conclusions leave little hope for minority schemes.

Despite the apparent limited influence of the worker representatives, man- agement generally is strongly opposed to minority representation on boards of directors. This opposition can partly be explained by a fear for parity representation as a next step, also the possible use by trade unions of secret information is highly resisted in management circles. Reports exist in both Germany and Norway about possible management manipulation of the workers' board representatives. Meetings of the other board members be- fore the official one, secrecy about a number of issues (e.g. salaries of directors), and rigging the meeting's agenda are reported in the Norwegian press (Arbeiderbladet, October 18, 1974). Wilpert states on this issue:

'. . . informal decision making procedures are established which dislocate the actual deci- sions into informal contacts and bargaining groups outside and prior to the board meetings

7. This study was originally published in Norwegian in 1964.

where the act of decision is degraded to a mere formality. The differential starting position of employee and owner representatives to obtain the relevant information from management might often disadvantage one or the other group (usually the employee side) in the process, in spite of the parity provisions'.
(Wilpert, 1973, 12-13).

The Norwegian Cooperation Project underlined the strong management preference for 'shop floor democracy' over board representation schemes. This is also supported by Wilkinson who surveyed 35 West European companies which were engaged in job redesign experiments of various sorts. Wilkinson (1970, 11) reported that 'almost universally the employers questioned held the opinion that steps toward true democracy could be better achieved by *local* involvement in *task* management of the worker who was expected to carry out the task, rather than by some remote union official sitting on the Board of Directors purporting to represent the workers.'

Summarizing this discussion on board representation it can be stated that this type of representation did open up a new range of organizational decisions which clearly involve the workers' long term interests. The actual ability of the worker representatives to influence these decisions is highly limited. Because of the nature of the decisions, the claim by some unions that the worker representatives on the board should be union officials seems to be justified. The issues dicussed at the board level seem to have more direct impact on general economic developments than on particular day-to-day company problems. A grasp of the more macro impact of certain decisions can probably better be evaluated by officials of a national union than by worker representatives from the company's shop floor. The interests of the latter representatives seem to be centered around decisions which are taken at a lower level within the organization.[8] Finally board representation can be evaluated in terms of the earlier presented definition of industrial democracy.

Table 13. Board representation.

domain	:	Restricted to decisions regarding major company policies (financing, expansion, closures, external relations).
weight	:	Important in particular from a long-term job security point of view.
strength	:	Low probability that decisional outcomes can be determined by the worker representatives.

8. In the next chapter a number of studies will be presented which support this assertion.

Corporate assembly representation

The Norwegian experience with the 1972 legislation providing for such a body with 1/3 worker representation is still too limited. A priori there is no reason to assume that the corporate assembly experiences should differ substantially from those of board representation.

Work and department councils

Work councils are committees with little or no decision making powers on which directly elected worker representatives have a majority position. In most West European countries the primary function of the work council is to facilitate communications and to allow workers' opinion to be expressed (Dufty, 1973, 33). Work councils are based upon a cooperation model of labor-management relations. They fall into that category of labor-management institutions which Blanpain (1974, 18) characterizes as follows: 'only the blind will not see that some of the European models of 'participation, tend to promote the collaboration of the employer and his employees'. In those countries where unions have only weak representation on the shop floor the work council functions somewhat as a local union substitute. The work council provides under those circumstances a forum where management and elected worker representatives can meet each other.

In Norway the work council is established by the Basic Agreement LO/ NAF, but outside Scandinavia work councils are generally introduced by national legislation. The work and department councils in Norway are somewhat integrated with the union local. The local union president and vice-president are ex-officio members of the work council and shop stewards are often represented in the department council. The goal of these councils is to promote labor-management cooperation at the enterprise level. The councils do not have any decision making power and are merely consultative to management.[9] Formally, issues like the economic and financial condition of the company, social matters, and education and training problems are to be discussed in these councils, but in practice all daily problems of the work situation are brought up by the worker representatives (Ryste, 1973* (b)). Issues related to wages and job classification cannot be discussed in the councils. As indicated in Chapter 2 the injection of union representation

9. For a more detailed presentation of the activities of these councils in Norway see Chapter 2, p. 27.

seems to have activated the councils in a number of companies. However the consensus still is that in the majority of companies the plant and department councils are not very active institutions.

Table 14. Work and department councils.

domain	:	Restricted; wage and wage related issues explicitly excluded. In practice shop floor complaints can be brought up.
weight	:	Complaints from the shop floor are generally considered very important by the workers.
strength	:	Councils have very limited decision making powers; on most issues only consultation takes place.

The shop steward system

In Norway the rights and obligations of the shop stewards are regulated in the Basic Agreement LO/NAF. The shop stewards are recognized as the official representatives and spokesmen of the organized workers. The role of the Norwegian shop steward in dealing with workers' complaints is much less specified than in the U.S. grievance procedure. Two excerpts from the Basic Agreement give an adequate impression of the type and character of the role of the shop steward in a typical Norwegian plant: 'Shop stewards have the right to take up and seek to settle amicably any grievances of the individual workers against the undertaking, or of the undertaking against the individual worker.' 'When the shop stewards have a question to discuss, they shall communicate directly with the employer or his representative at the place of work' (LO/NAF, 1974*, 10-12).

The effectiveness of this more informal approach towards grievance handling seems to be generally underestimated by Anglo-Saxon observers of the Scandinavian industrial relations systems. Particularly in the larger companies with a well developed union local and shop steward system the influence of the shop stewards on the settling of day-to-day complaints is considerable. In addition the shop steward with special responsibilities in the health and safety area has the right to stop the production process if he considers it dangerous for the workers. The shop steward plays an important role in linking the different forms to attain industrial democracy to the shop floor workers. He is generally a member of the plant bargaining committee, and sits on the department council, in addition to which he represents both the local union, the national union, and LO at the shop floor.

Table 15. The shop steward system.

domain	:	Issues of immediate relevance to the shop floor (complaints, grievances).
weight	:	These issues are considered very important by shop floor workers.
strength	:	Restricted formal powers but reasonable influence to determine certain decision making outcomes.

Democratization of work and job regulation

Through redesign of the work organization workers can be given more influence on decisions directly related to their tasks. In addition increased worker influence on a number of personnel issues and regulations regarding working conditions can be attained (see e.g. Norsk Medisinaldepot). These changes are examples of direct, participatory democracy. Increased democracy through job redesign can be called work democratization, while increased control over personnel matters can be labeled democratization of job regulation. Democratization of job regulation takes place if decisions regarding hours of work (e.g. flexi-time), election of supervisor, selection of new employees etc. are made by the workers themselves. Work and job regulation democratization only occurs if, and only if:

1. The workers and their representatives influence the decisions during the change process.
2. The changes lead to increased worker autonomy at the job.
3. The workers share in the possible economic benefits of the changes.
4. The workers evaluate the complex of changes positively.

If these four conditions are not met job redesign is nothing more than an unilateral management introduction of a new type of work organization. Only a few cases are known at present where all these four necessary conditions have been fulfilled. The Norwegian experiments have shown that management generally initiates and controls the redesign process, only a few cases support the here presented argument that changes can be introduced which lead to increased democracy despite the overwhelming number of constraining factors.

Table 16. Democratization of work and job regulation.

domain	:	Issues related to the immediate task and regulation of work.
weight	:	Important.
strength	:	On certain of these issues workers can fully determine decision making outcomes.

The preceeding presentation of the forms to attain industrial democracy, which are used in Norway, underlines that these different approaches generally aim at different issues at different levels in the industrial relations system. A possible exception to this argument is the work council. The work council is probably superfluous in organizations with a strong union local and a well developed shop steward system. On the other hand it can be argued that the work council provides a forum where management and elected worker representatives can meet on issues of an integrative nature. The forms to attain industrial democracy which are presented here cover the complete range of industrial relations' issues (domain) that are of interest to the workers (weight). The low probability that workers can determine the decisional outcomes (strength), with the possible exception of collective bargaining, means that they only modestly contribute to industrial democracy. The managerial prerogative on a wide range of organizational issues is still very real. Even despite this fact most forms supplement collective bargaining in Norway in a very useful manner. All forms to increase industrial democracy, except for work democratization, are representative. Representative systems are useful in improving the general conditions of work. They are not designed however to take account of the nature of each individual's task. Work democratization through job design is indeed the only form whereby direct control and participation of the worker is possible. The argument between Clegg (1960), advocating representative democracy, and Blumberg (1968), arguing in favor of participatory democracy, is therefore superfluous.

The approaches are not mutually exclusive but support each other. Job redesign attempts to change technology and the organizational control system, areas which have been rather neglected by the representative approaches. The representative approaches fulfill basically a controlling function while work democratization provides for participatory democracy within a certain restricted area. A job redesign project can only be successful if it is linked in its different phases to the collective bargaining process. The shelter agreement in the beginning and bargaining about the changed work effort relation in a later phase cannot adequately be dealt with by only those who are immediately involved. This is one example where two approaches to industrial democracy supplement each other.

The collective bargaining process by itself is not adequately equipped to deal with work democratization (see Chapter 4). U.S. unions generally do not favor the council type of committees and work democratization projects on the ground that the union should be the only organization representing the workers. Representation and active participation are not the same however and must be recognized as such. The attitude of the U.S. union must of course be seen in the context of the more antagonistic labor-management relations in the U.S. and the low degree of unionization (approximately 30%). Different approaches in the U.S. could relieve the 'overburdened'[10] bargaining process.

Theoretically, issues like unemployment benefits, health insurance, and pensions could be dealt with by legislation and issues like requests for protective gloves, sweatbands, and a different quality of toilet paper could be delegated to more informal forms like a work council. The completely different political and industrial relations environment in the U.S. make such proposals highly irrelevant from a practical perspective. It can be maintained however that collective bargaining is not the ideal form to solve all issues regarding industrial democracy. As mentioned here, work democratization is complementary. Other forms could also complement the bargaining process. Cole (1957, 14) stated some of the limitations of bargaining as follows:

'Trade union bargaining, though of utmost value in dealing with such matters as standard wage rates, working hours, and generally applicable conditions of employment, is by no means well adapted for dealing with the host of *particular* issues that arise in *particular* work places and are of most immediate concern to the individual worker and the face-to-face working group.'[11]

Collective bargaining simply cannot be a substitute for work democratization and forms of representation at a level directly accessible to the workers themselves.

One severe limitation of the above analysis of industrial democracy is its

10. This term was used by Irving Bluestone in an interview in September 1974.
11. Italics mine.

relative neglect of all informal procedures and methods to advance the worker interest. Particularly in a U.S. – Norway comparison the emphasis on formal aspects and contractual rights could easily lead to underestimate the impact of the more informal nature of some Norwegian industrial democracy forms. Informal methods unfortunately do not easily lend themselves for any kind of institutional analysis.

The package approach towards industrial democracy as described here is quickly gaining ground in West European trade union circles. The 1971 program on industrial democracy adopted by the Swedish LO congress can be credited with being the first formulation of a package oriented policy (LO (Sweden), 1972). This program of the Swedish LO proposes board representation mainly for the purposes of observation, but the observations are to be fed back to collective bargaining and the work council. The powers of the work council should be increased so that the council can deal rather autonomously with planning, staffing, training and related issues. Work democratization through job design is endorsed as a method to increase the level of autonomy in the jobs of the individual workers. Collective bargaining should be strengthened in order to deal with the wages and working conditions. Finally legislation is proposed to limit the managerial prerogative as defined by the famous paragraph 32 of the Constitution of the Swedish Employers Federation (SAF). In Norway no such specific LO program exists, but top leaders in interviews clearly expressed the strategies of the Norwegian labor movement in similar terms. The action program of the European Trade Union Confederation (ETUC) also endorses a package approach in order to achieve industrial democracy within the membership countries of the EEC.

An unanswered question remains. At which level are the most important decisions being made within the industrial relations system? Berle and Means' (1934) argument that power had shifted from the stockholders to top management seems fairly well accepted today. Galbraith (1968) extended this argument and identified the techno-structure as the most important group within modern organizations. The power of the techno-structure is based upon specialized knowledge and expertise. If the power indeed rests with the techno-structure the acquisition by the labor movements in Europe of board representation could be some kind of empty victory. This issue of where the power is located can better be approached from the point of view of each individual decision. The place where a particular decision is made can be identified, hereafter means to influence this decision can be chosen. The strong reaction of unions against the multi-national companies and the unions' attempts to organize international countervailing organizations is an example of a development of such a new means for control. Advocates of job redesign in Western Europe generally propose decentralization within unions in order to deal better with the issues of work organization (e.g. Thorsrud, 1973(b)). This is a legitimate suggestion. However the increasing size of corporations and the growth of multi-national undertakings require even more centralization. Here again the solution is a differentation by the type of decisions or issues. Unions could decentralize with respect to issues regarding shop floor organization and at the same time centralize at a European or possibly world level around issues concerned with the multi-national undertaking. The danger of undifferentiated decentralization is in a somewhat exagerated manner stated by the German trade unionist Cieslak: 'The theory of participatory democracy leads in practice to decentralization and isolation of the separate parts and levels of the labor movement. The highly centralized and concentrated power of capital and the state can not be effectively challenged in this manner.' (Cieslak, 1972*, 166).

The interrelationships between the different approaches to achieve industrial democracy are very difficult to describe in general terms. In particular the integration between those forms which are primarily geared to deal with issues of an integrative nature (work councils) and collective bargaining is a difficult problem. The Norwegian experience shows that the shop steward system can play an important role in linking these two forms. The advantage of the existence of a number of different approaches gives the unions and the workers a measure of choice in selecting that particular form which best fits local problems and circumstances. It is obvious that there is no company in Norway where all the here presented forms are simultaneously utilized to any significant extent. It is however a measure of progress that through collective bargaining, legislation, and cooperation between LO/ NAF a number of different approaches are developed which all can be of potential use. The enforcement of general schemes of industrial democracy is virtually impossible given the wide diversity of organizations and organizational members. The 'package approach' provides at this point in time a measure of choice between different approaches towards industrial democracy.

Industrial democracy is defined here as 'the extent to which workers or their representatives influence the outcome of organizational decisions'. In most of the approaches towards industrial democracy, with the exception of collective bargaining, the workers or their representatives do not have the necessary strength (power) to determine the decisional outcomes. The work council in Norway e.g. does not have any power to make decisions, it is purely consultative in nature. Management power can be based upon: 1. legitimacy; 2. reward and sanction control; 3. expertise; 4. personal liking (charisma); and 5. coercion. (Filley and House, 1969).

Participation in decision making without adequate powers does not necessarily lead to increased industrial democracy. Emery and Thorsrud's (1969) study of board representation demonstrated the difficult position of the worker representatives on the board. Their minority position and lacking expertise resulted in their 'cooptation' by the rest of the board members. Mulder (1971, 1972*) in a number of laboratory and field experiments empirically tested and accepted the hypothesis that 'When there are relatively large differences in the expert powers of members of a system, an increase in participation will increase the power difference' (Mulder, 1971, 34). How large these differences in expert power must be, remains an unanswered question but Mulder's creative research provides an important warning from the point of view of industrial democracy. Mulder (1972*) demonstrates that not only expertise but also the other above listed power bases can create situations where participation leads to increased power differences. Again this does not mean that these forms to increase industrial democracy, where there are substantial power differences, should be rejected. Their limitations should be recognized. Selznick (1969, 117) underwrites the need of adequate power when he states that effective participation is only possible with 'organizational support and must therefore be founded in latent power'. It is the union organization which can provide this latent support under those forms of worker representation where large power differences exist between management and worker representatives. Zupanov in this context contends that the assumption of an equal distribution of power could have detrimental effects from the worker point of view: 'should the assumption of an even distribution of power fail to materialize, the lack of regulations with regard to the use of power opens the door to excesses and abuses in its exercise'. (Zupanov, 1973, 216).

To avoid possible manipulations in job redesign, the boundary conditions within which job redesign can take place, must be agreed upon in a collective agreement (the shelter agreement). There are of course influence processes going on in work councils and board of directors which are not based upon the use of one of the power bases. However in critical situations relative power differences will be the deciding factor. Therefore the here cited studies suggest that within a hierarchical production organization the voice of those at the bottom of the hierarchy can be more freely and effectively expressed when backed by an organization (union) independent of the hierarchy of the production organization and ultimately by their collective strength to compensate for the power those at the bottom lack in the latter organization.

Participatory democracy within an enterprise naturally has its limitations. These limitations fall into two broad categories: 1. individual limitations; and 2. structural limitations. The basic question underlying the first limitation is: to what extent do workers want increased participation in their immediate task environment? This question has only received limited attention in the literature. The structural limitations center around the question: to what extent is participatory democracy in conflict with the division of labor, the essence of organizational efficiency?

It is well supported that workers prefer participation in their immediate task environment over participation in broader organizational issues.[12] How strong the desire to participate in this area and how broad its scope, is largely an unanswered question. The following quote from Supek describing the dynamics of workers' self-management in Yugoslavia provides some insights into the possible individual limitations of participatory democracy:

'It (worker self-management) is always greatest at the beginning, after its introduction, and afterwards slows down gradually, becoming a routine activity, in which the technical problems of running business predominate over problems of participation of the members and social problems in general. Probably this rule holds for all newly formed institutions of a democratic character, because in the beginning the participation of the members of a community is greater and afterwards it slows down and becomes more a matter of routine. This behavior could be observed in our whole social system (Yugoslavia) from the war up to the present. That would mean that every democratic institution, and therefore also institutions of direct democracy, are subjected to a time dynamic in the sense that participation is greater at the beginning and then becomes more passive, routine, takes on perhaps a more defensive character. This can be seen from the fact that in *critical* situations participation again becomes very intensive.'
(Supek, 1970, 231).

A similar dynamic is evident in the voluntary attendance to trade union meetings. This attendance generally is minimal unless there is an issue to be decided that is defined as critical by the workers, e.g. a strike. It could be that advocates of participatory democracy (e.g. Pateman, 1970) overestimate the individual's desire to participate in a wide range of organizational decisions. The Norwegian job design experiments however show that in organizations workers will after an introductory period respond positively to opportunities for increased participation in the immediate work setting. The limits of the individual's desire to participate do not yet seem to be reached in these experiments.

12. Chapter 6 includes a summary of these studies.

Michels (1958) in his well known *Political Parties* summarized many of the structural limitations of participatory democracy in his 'iron law of oligarchy'. He reasoned that participatory democracy of all organizational members in determining major organizational policies is impossible for mechanical and technical reasons. This holds in particular for large organizations. It is often imperative that decisions be made quickly and decisively, thus limiting the number of organizational members who can participate in decision making. Michels used this argument to explain the need for centralized, autocratic leadership in political parties. In addition to these dynamics, an enterprise needs to meet certain minimum levels of productivity and efficiency. Specialization and the division of labor plus the economies of scale are the main reasons for the modern enterprises' efficiency and productivity. At some point in a development towards participatory democracy compromises must be made between participation and the need for specialized skills, and between participatory democracy in small units and economies of scale (Tinbergen, 1970, 117). A caveat similar like the one concluding the discussion of the individual limitation is in order. The changes which increased worker autonomy and participation in the Norwegian experiments by no means conflicted with productivity, on the contrary productivity generally increased significantly. It can therefore be concluded that with respect to the current developments in work democratization the structural and individual limitations on participatory democracy are only of theoretical interest. Almost all experiments in job redesign which increase participation and worker autonomy show that no changes are being implemented which hamper productivity or efficiency. The dominant management position within enterprises just would not allow for it. There are evidently limits to participatory democracy, but these limits have certainly not been reached in the Norwegian experiments. The existence of these limits is another argument in favor of representative forms to increase industrial democracy. In those decision making areas where no direct participatory control is possible, control can only be exercised by representative bodies.

The Webbs (1902) already warned that democracy within an undertaking does not automatically assure adequate attention to the broader public interest. The methods to further industrial democracy which have been presented here are all of a bilateral (management – employees) nature. Developments in industrialized countries over the last decades show an increasing governmental role in industrial relations as the defender of the public interest. A next step in the democratization process of the enterprise in Europe will very likely be the direct formal injection of this public interest in the

organizational decision-making process (Bolweg and Weisz, 1974). In Norway, Sweden and Denmark plans already exist which propose the representation of the community and the broader public interests on the board of
directors. Norwegian trade union leaders expect the next step to be the introduction of public interest representatives in the corporate assembly and the
board of directors. Employee representation in these organs would be reduced from one-third to one-fourth, while the public interest would also be
represented by one-fourth of the total number of representatives. An increase
of employees plus public interest representatives to more than half is very
unlikely, in that this is in conflict with the Norwegian constitution. These
proposals put industrial democracy into a larger framework of societal democracy. In the very long run conflicts between these developments and the
political democratic system could become a reality (Halverson in interview,
1974).

Job redesign can supplement the more traditional forms to attain industrial
democracy in an area where these forms generally have been deficient: the
immediate job setting. Industrial democracy is not a question of indirect
control (Clegg, 1960) or direct participation (Blumberg, 1968; Emery and
Thorsrud, 1969), but a matter of indirect control through representation,
with collective bargaining as its most powerful form, *and* direct participation. Changes in job design can, if certain conditions are met, contribute to
industrial democracy. Job redesign can only be labeled work democratization if workers and their representatives influence the redesign process, if
the changes lead to increased autonomy of the workers, if the workers share
in the possible economic benefits of the changes, and if they afterwards
evaluate the changes as positive. Work democratization can introduce some
measure of participatory democracy into an enterprise. Because of its participatory and individual nature work democratization is as yet not very well
integrated into trade union practice. Union organizational support is however necessary to provide the workers with a degree of latent power in the redesign process. Job redesign aims mainly at changing the organizational control system and technology at the lower organizational levels. Despite the
fact that the managerial prerogative is directly linked to the organizational
control system management generally seems to prefer changes in job design
over the other forms to increase industrial democracy. This could be an indication that these changes are perceived as less threatening to organizational
efficiency and the managerial prerogative.

The other presented forms to attain industrial democracy – legislation,
collective bargaining, board representation, work and department councils,

and shop steward system – all present indirect, representative approaches. It is argued that these forms plus work democratization are not mutually exclusive but that together they can increase worker influence in different decisions at different organizational and even supra-organizational levels. This simultaneous use of these different forms has been called the 'package approach' towards industrial democracy. This type of approach is increasingly advocated and practiced by West European trade unions (L.O. (Sweden), 1972; ETUC, 1974). Some of the limitations of the different forms towards industrial democracy were also presented in this chapter.

6. A broader perspective and conclusions

OVERVIEW
Job design and the quality of working life – is there a need for job redesign? – opposing views reconciled – job consciousness – labor market and legitimacy – recent developments in Norway – Cooperation Project evaluated – conditions for accelerated implementation – participatory democracy: utopia?

The changes in job design which were presented so far in a framework of industrial democracy can also be placed in the context of the quality of working life, humanization of work, job structuring, and work improvement discussions. In all industrialized countries we are witnessing a fast growing interest in job redesign. The quality of working life, humanization of work, job structuring, work improvement, and work democratization all have as their major thrust: to make work more interesting and challenging through the redesign of jobs and work organization. Job redesign is the keystone in approaches to reduce fragmentation and specialization in work, to eliminate as far as possible dull and demeaning work, and to change the 'anachronistic authoritarianism' (H.E.W., 1973, XVI) of the work place.

The underlying value premise of those advocating job redesign is that a large part of the work in our industrial societies is of a routine, dull and unchallenging nature. The second premise is that many of these jobs through redesign can be changed in such a manner that the human factor in work becomes more than a mere appendage to a machine. As Delamotte and Walker (1974) correctly point out the commodity theory of labor and the machine approach to human work had been under criticism, in particular from the side of trade unions, long before current strands of thought emerged under the labels of the quality of working life and the humanization of work. The humanization of work not only includes job design as a means to provide for more meaninlful and satisfying work with increased participation in decisions affecting the work situation, it also includes attempts to humanize the physical working environment, the wage-effort bargain, and the protection of the worker against the hazards of illness and unemployment, and against the exercise of arbitrary authority (Delamotte and Walker, 1974, 4). The main thrust of the Norwegian Cooperation Project was job redesign and we will therefore continue to focus primarily on this one aspect of the humanization of work and the quality of working life.

The number of organizations and institutions that have job redesign as their main goal is growing rapidly and it will suffice here to give only a few examples. In Norway and Sweden we find national labor-management councils for the advancement of industrial democracy through job redesign. In the Netherlands, United Kingdom, France, and Australia recently substantial government funds have been made available for institutes and practical experimentation in this area. In the United States the Quality of Working Life Center at U.C.L.A. and the National Quality of Work Center at the University of Michigan's Institute of Social Research are the first institutes which have the redesign of jobs as their major field of interest. At the International level the Organization for Economic Cooperation and Development (O.E.C.D.) has been very instrumental in the dissemination of the new job design principles.[1] The 1972 Arden House conference on the Quality of Working Life resulted in the establishment of an International Council for the Quality of Working Life which has as its main function the exchange of information and experiences in this area. Another indicator of growing interest in job redesign is the continuous stream of visitors, many of them from the United States, to Sweden and Norway for the study of some of the Scandinavian accomplishments. Finally the number of field experiments is rapidly expanding in almost all industrialized countries (see e.g. H.E.W., 1973, 188-201; Jenkins, 1973 and 1974).

All these developments could leave one with the false impression that a general consensus exists about the necessity of these attempts to create more interesting and challenging work. On the contrary there are a number of serious controversies and some difficulty to reconcile empirical social science findings in this areas.[2] First there is the consistent reporting of generally high

1. In addition to its work on social indicators, the internal industrial environment and industrial relations, the O.E.C.D. recently has been responsible for the following specific activities in this area: 1. Revans, R. W. *The Emerging Attitudes and Motivations of Workers*. Paris: O.E.C.D., 1972. 2. International Conference on New Patterns for Working Time (September, 1972). 3. Regional Joint Seminar on Prospects for Labour-Management Cooperation in the Enterprise (October, 1972). 4. Management Seminar on Advances in Work Organization (April, 1973). 5. Management Experts' Meeting on Absenteeism and Labour Turnover (October, 1973). 6. Regional Trade Union Seminar on the Quality of Life at the Workplace (May, 1974). 7. International Conference on Work in a Changing Industrial Society (October, 1974). 8. Joint Experts' Meeting on Some Aspects of the Industrial Environment of Work (December, 1974). 9. Management Seminar on Workers' Participation (March, 1975).
2. In support of each argument only one or two relevant studies are mentioned here. It is

job satisfaction among the work forces of the industrialized countries (Barbash, 1974(a)). For the U.S. a recent monograph by the Department of Labor analyzing longitudinal data concluded that there is no conclusive evidence of a dramatic decline in job satisfaction. This study showed that between 1958 and 1973 the percentage of satisfied workers in the U.S. labor force fluctuated between 81% and 92% (U.S. Department of Labor, 1973, 4). A 1972 representative sample of 2262 LO members in Norway also showed a high percentage of satisfied workers. In this survey 95% of the respondents were very satisfied or satisfied, 12% were neither satisfied nor dissatisfied, while only 3% were dissatisfied or very dissatisfied (Karlsen, 1972*, 41). Fein (1973(a)) concludes from these satisfaction percentages that there is no urgent need for job redesign.

Those supporting job redesign reject this argument and counter job satisfaction studies with empirical studies showing high alienation among certain groups of industrial workers (Sheppard and Herrick, 1972; H.E.W., 1973). They reject Fein's interpretation of the findings of job satisfaction studies and postulate adaptive worker responses to work, the high degree of ego involvement in work, and the lack of alternative experiences for workers which could change their current expectations as the explanations for the reported high job satisfaction (Cherns and Davis, 1975). Despite high job satisfaction only a few in Western Europe would reject the following analysis by a well known French sociologist: 'Nobody wants to be an industrial worker . . . if you are a young man and go to work in an industry you are considered a marginal man . . . . The industrial culture is disappearing . . . When people have choice they move from the industrial organization to the tertiary system' (Quoted in Barbash, 1974(a), 22). The question remains however whether or not high percentages of satisfied workers are a sufficient reason to retain the existing forms of work organization?

A second related discussion centers around the interpretation of the behavioral indices of job satisfaction. Increased management concern is reported about rising absenteeism and turnover. This concern is supported by national statistics of rising quit rates and absenteeism in a number of industrialized countries (O.E.C.D., 1973(a)). In addition some Norwegian and Swedish employers are facing recruitment problems for unattractive jobs. Do the quit rates and absenteeism statistics reflect the need for job redesign? No, concludes a recent U.S. study which confirmed increased absenteeism and turnover (Flanagan et al., 1974) because the increases can be satis-

not the purpose of the following section to provide a comprehensive overview of all studies used in the discussions.

factorally explained by changes in the demographic composition of the labor force. The proportion of the work force of groups with high quit and absentee rates (women, blacks, and young workers) has risen.

A third controversy centers around the interpretation of the dominant worker attitude to work. Studies by Goldthorpe and his associates (1969) and the reanalysis by Fein (1973(a)) of the H.E.W. data, support, for blue collar workers at least, the existence of a predominant instrumental attitude to work. Goldthrope et al. (1969, 38-39) discount the importance of work itself for the workers and state: 'The primary meaning of work is as a means to an end, or, ends, external to the work situation; that is, work is regarded as a means necessary to support a valued way of life of which work itself is not an integral part'. The U.S. unionist Winpisinger (1973, 9) underscribes this conclusion in a more blunt manner: 'if you want to enrich the job, enrich the pay check'. Proponents of job redesign do not question Goldthorpe's findings but argue that it is exactly the lack of any intrinsically satisfying work experiences that contributes to these instrumental attitudes. Only experiences with more challenging and interesting work will cultivate a taste for it. Some support for this argument was provided here in the analysis of the Norwegian experiments.

Finally, a lack of consensus exists whether or not fragmented and specialized work has an impact upon personal characteristics and activities outside the place of work. Kohn and Schooler (1973) in a very careful analysis report the following relationship between the extent to which a worker controls his job and certain personal characteristics: 'The evidence constantly suggests that although men undoubtedly do choose and mold their jobs to fit their personal requirements, it is not likely that these processes alone can sufficiently explain occupational conditions and psychological functioning' (Kohn and Schooler, 1973, 109). Meissner (1971) finds support for the position that workers in highly specialized jobs are less active in their leisure activities than those which have less specialized jobs. His research clearly points to a carry-over effect from work experience to leisure activities. The opposing view with respect to the impact of work on the worker and his leisure activities is that leisure activities adequately compensate for the strain, stress, or lack of challenge on the job. Work is not very central to the life interests of the workers. The central life interest of workers is centered around his non-work activities. The latter reflects Wilensky's (1960) compensatory hypothesis, which involves 'explosive compensation for the deadening rhythms of factory life'. The spillover hypothesis refers to the situation where mental stultification produced by work permeates leisure. Parker (1972) reports empirical studies supporting both hypotheses.

Scepticism and concern is also generally found among trade union leaders, with the possible exception of Norwegian and Swedish unionists, who fear that ameliorating the quality of working life is another underhanded means to improve productivity and weaken the benefits the unions have won on behalf of their members. Unionists fear that job redesign is a new manipulative tool to get more work out of workers without appropriate remuneration; that it is designed to deflect workers from making wage demands by increasing intrinsic rewards in work; that job redesign is an attempt to reduce worker attachment to their unions by making them more satisfied; or that it is designed to generate the illusion of greater worker control at the same as reducing the substance by giving workers a greater say over unimportant decisions, thereby deflecting their attention from the bigger and more important decisions.

There is little doubt that increased productivity and cost reduction are the underlying interests of management in job redesign and the quality of working life. Adequate worker control in the redesign phases can sufficiently counterbalance this management interest however. The management interest in the productivity aspects of job redesign points to the necessity of differentiation between the job design principles as proposed in the quality of working life literature and the practical implementation of these principles at the company level. The earlier presented Nobø case is one of several examples where the job redesign process was not adequately controlled by the workers. Worker control over the redesign process is necessary to reduce the chances for worker manipulation. Both trade unionism and the quality of working life literature reject the commodity theory of labor and both do contribute to the goal of making the conditions of work more suitable to the human aspects of the labor factor.

This brief presentation of the opposing views with respect to the necessity of job redesign gives an impression of the unclear picture which presents itself to policy makers in this area. It also reflects an inherent weakness of social science research which leaves its findings open to so many different interpretations. The use of different research paradigms, e.g. the job satisfaction and alienation paradigms, leads to seemingly opposing interpretations with respect to the necessity of job redesign. Job satisfaction research is interpreted as evidence that there is no problem in this area (Fein, 1973(a)), while alienation research findings (H.E.W., 1973) can be interpreted as pointing to a clear need for changes in our organizational structures. An inherent weakness of the descriptive social science studies is its reliance upon data from existing organizations. This in itself is a strong argument in favor of longterm, carefully monitored, experimentation in organizational and job redesign. Whether or not to support job redesign experiments is basically a political decision based upon a subjective value assessment whether industrial and service sector jobs need improvements or not.

In this study the endorsement of job redesign experiments has been obvious. This does not imply however 'the prospect that work can be self-actualizing for everybody, or almost everybody' (Barbash, 1974(b), 22). Endorsement of the new job design principles means that efforts should be made to make work as attractive and challenging as practically possible. Working out of necessity in a somewhat more intrinsically satisfying manner has been proven possible in an increasing number of different organizational circumstances. Unnecessary polarization, which is particularly evident in the U.S., France, and Belgium, hampers the changes for new experiments in re-designing jobs.

One area of the quality of working life discussion which is unnecessarily polarized is the question raised earlier: what is the 'true' worker interest in work? A simple solution to the controversy could be that both pay and interesting work are important to the worker. The experiments reported so far do not suggest any necessary trade-off between pay and more interesting work. The Norwegian projects even suggest that the outcome of job re-design can be both- slightly increased pay and somewhat more interesting work. The findings of Daniel[3] seem to support the thesis that workers are interested in both pay and interesting work; but that their relevance is not the same in different contexts (Daniel, 1970; Daniel and McIntosh, 1972). Daniel develops a contingency model of worker interest and finds subsequent support for it in his studies of productivity bargaining in a number of British companies. Workers, following Daniel's argument, have different sets of priorities that relate to different stituations and contexts. He distinguishes between two major contexts: the negotiation context and the operating context (the day-to-day work situation). In the negotiation context, which includes both the job searching process and collective bargaining, the level of income is the dominating worker interest. In these situations considerations of job satisfaction and interesting work are irrelevant. The worker is here only interested in making the best financial deal for himself. In the case of collective bargaining, the interests more closely related to the nature of work become only prevalent *after* the agreement is settled. In the negotiating and work situations:

3. For a brief introduction to his research see Daniel (1972).

'the worker is interested in very different things . . . Indeed his priorities are completely reversed and the implicit concepts of work reflected in these, respectively, are logically opposing and quite inconsistent. The concept of work and change expressed in the negotiating context (productivity bargaining) is that more work and change are pure disutility for the worker, so he must be compensated handsomely for accepting them. In the operating context, however, the implicit definition of work is that it is potentially interesting and rewarding in its own right, and that more work can bring about increased satisfaction and intrinsic rewards'.

(Daniel, 1972, 585).

The following quote from a Danish worker participating in a job redesign project seems to support the idea of the two different contexts: 'The firm is a profit oriented enterprise, and we only come here for the sake of money, but that does not keep us from making our daily work as pleasant as possible' (Quoted in Agersnap et al., 1974, 40). Daniel and McIntosh (1972, 40-42) found in their studies of productivity bargaining that the acceptance of a productivity agreement depends only on the prospects of increased earnings. However, the resulting changes in job design, which provided for increased intrinsic rewards in work, were at a later stage very much appreciated by the workers.

Daniel's findings are clearly in line with the here proposed joint management-union-worker process of job redesign which is anchored to collective bargaining by a shelter agreement and a kind of ex-post productivity bargaining. Daniel's model can also be used for a possible explanation of initial worker resistance to job redesign. This initial resistance can be based upon fear for losing income and job security (the negotiating context) followed by the later positive evaluation of the changes (the operating context). The identification of the collective bargaining context with monetary interests should caution trade unionists like Winpisinger (1972) in their conclusion about what workers really want. In the collective bargaining context workers surely express merely demands for increased wages and job security, but it is possible that worker interests with respect to the operating context are not always adequately articulated. Bluestone underlines the complementary of the extrinsic and intrinsic rewards from work when he states: 'While his (the worker's) rate of pay may predominate his relationship to his job, he can be responsive to the opportunity for playing an innovative, creative, and imaginative role in the production process' (Bluestone, 1972(a), 4). This evaluation is more balanced than the assumptions regarding worker interests which we find either in Winpisinger (1972) and Fein (1973(a)) as proponents of pure instrumentalism or the self-actualization position of organizational theorists like Likert (1961) and McGregor (1960).

An argument in favor of job redesign is that it involves the immediate work situation. This is the area which is of the most direct interest to workers and also the area over which they want more control. Perlman argued already in 1928 that workers are much more interested in matters relating to their direct job setting than in larger organizational issues. In his own words:

'To the working man, the freedom that matters supremely is the freedom on the job, freedom from unjust discrimination, which enables him to face his boss 'man to man'. Compared with this tangible sort of freedom, the higher 'freedom', the freedom to elect the managers of industry who are to supplant the present day private boss, or the freedom which the intellectual talks about, appears too remote to enter into actual calculation'.
(Perlman, 1928, 290).

Applying Perlman's arguments today, one would predict a more potent workers' interest in work democratization than in representation on the board of directors. The list of emprical studies which support this contention is steadily growing.[4] Holter (1965) reported from a questionnaire investigation among 1128 workers and staff-members in Norway that 56% of the workers and 67% of the staff-members would like increased participation in decisions directly related to their own work situation. Only 16% of the workers and 11% of the staff-members preferred more participation in decisions concerning general company matters. Another questionnaire study carried out in the Netherlands by the Central Work Council of Philips also indicated that workers wanted extended influence in issues close to the job. The following issues were ranked as most important: transfers, composition of work group, appointment of supervisor, evaluation, work preparation, task allocation inside the work group and individual training and education (Philips, 1973*, 16). Lawler (1968) in a job enlargement literature review concluded that worker participation in matters directly related to the work process has a considerably stronger impact on worker motivation than participation involving matters of general company policy. Van Zuthem (1973*) reports a number of Dutch studies which also indicate that workers' desire to participate is considerably larger in issues in which they are more directly involved. He summarizes that the 'workers' desire for participation does not actually challenge the existing power hierarchy' (Van Zuthem, 1973*, 181). Goldthorpe and his associates (Goldthorpe et al., 1969, 99 and 103) found in their Luton (U.K.) study that only 7% of the union members regularly attended branch meetings, while over 80% were active in union affairs at work shop level, where there was an opportunity to influence policy relating

4. See also Walker (1975) for a summary of these studies.

to the immediate task. Finally Form in a cross national study of automobile workers in the United States, Italy, Argentina, and India concludes 'that irrespective of the ideologies of their unions or their own personal politics, workers everywhere emphasize the principle of job-conscious unionism' (Form, 1973, 237).

Perlman's conclusions about the interests of the working man is clearly supported by recent empirical research. Job conscious unionism and work democratization, theoretically at least, are highly compatible. However the vested rights which job conscious unions have gained for their members will initially reinforce a strong resistance against changes in work organization (see e.g. the case of the Norwegian printers).

Pateman (1970) and other participatory democracy theorists maintain that it is the lack of freedom and participation at the shop floor which is responsible for this minimal worker interest in decision making at higher organizational levels:

'The evidence suggests that the low existing level of demand for higher level participation in the work place might, at least in part, be explained as an effect of a socialization process which, both through the notion of his role-to-be at work gained by the ordinary boy and through the experiences of the individual inside the work place, could lead to the idea of higher level participation being unavailable for many workers'.

(Pateman, 1970, 107).

Emery and Thorsrud's (1969) developmental model of industrial democracy is based on similar learning premises. The experiments in Norway provide very limited support for the theory that increased autonomy at the shop floor will lead to increased worker involvement in broader company affairs.

What the experiments showed more clearly was: 1. that increased autonomy at the shop floor combined with other changes in the work organization were evaluated positively by the workers despite initial resistance against such changes (the 'experience hypothesis'); 2. that changes beyond the immediate job redesign are severely constrained by the larger organization. No continuous change process developed in the Norwegian companies, the projects stagnated after a certain period of time. This stagnation or the lack of continuity seems to be a general characteristic of such experiments in job design (Van der Does, 1973, 80).

The recently started experiments in a number of Norwegian companies probably will reach a similar stagnation phase in particular where the goals of recent experiments are more limited: to increase productivity and improve the work situation in order to attract sufficient labor. Management in these companies does not envision any overall organizational change process to occur. In this respect the latest experiments in Norway resemble the developments in Sweden. It is clear that in most of those experiments the four conditions for industrial democracy are not met. A Swedish LO official with special responsibilities in the area of job redesign complained that most companies are interested only in limited forms of reorganization: 'When it comes to more far reaching expansion of the independence and competence of workers within companies, there is not so much interest' (Janerius, quoted in Jenkins, 1974, 28).

The findings of organizational psychologists in the are of individual differences should guard against too optimistic conclusions regarding workers' interests and abilities for more interesting and demanding work. Turner and Lawrence (1965) found that the urban versus rural background of workers explained some of the differences in behavior and attitudes towards more complex jobs. The city workers expressed more satisfaction with highly programmed undemanding work. Hulin and Blood (1968) used a measure of alienation from middle class values in successfully explaining some of the differences between successful and unsuccessful job enlargement-enrichment experiments. Hackman and Lawler (1971) found that a measure of the need for self actualization moderated both job content – worker satisfaction and job content – work motivation relationships.

This body of literature and the experiences from the Norwegian field projects indicate that there are indeed individual differences with respect to desire for and responses to more interesting and demanding work. Older workers and also young woman workers sometimes resist changes in job design. Some workers prefer a simple routine task, which can be performed automatically and almost unconsciously, and leaves them free to talk, gossip, and day dream. This is sometimes preferred over a more complex task that requires full attention. These preferences and individual differences should be respected as far as possible in job redesign projects.

The stringent labor market in Norway has been mentioned several times as the reason for the current interest in management circles in job redesign. The developments in the other industrialized countries of Western Europe, with unusually high unemployment rates (4%-5%), suggest that national aggregate unemployment is less important in triggering job redesign experiments than labor shortages in certain segments of the labor market. In addition to segmental labor shortages the industrialized countries of Western Europe are faced with increasing problems with respect to the substantial numbers of foreign workers from Southern Europe and North Africa. This results in a situation where both high unemployment and large numbers of foreign workers coincide. In the Netherlands in November 1974 there were 165,000 people registered as unemployed while at the same time 80,000 foreign workers were employed. In Dutch government circles job redesign is being considered as one possible method to reduce both unemployment and the number of foreign workers. Making jobs more attractive could theoretically reduce the number of nationals unemployed.

. Another context in which job redesign can be considered is the decentralizing trend in Western European industrial relations and the suggested decrease in legitimacy of the established management and union institutions at the company level. Schregle (1974) and Dufty (1973) agree on a decentralizing trend in collective bargaining, while Kassalow (1974) cites increased industrial unrest at the shop floor levels as an indicator of a need for change in the established management and union practices. Whether the downward trend in collective bargaining is a result of increased shop floor demands for a role in the rule determining processes or a response to certain macro economic developments (differential industry and company growth rates under high inflation conditions) is hard to establish.

The return in Norway in 1974 to industry bargaining without a national framework agreement is best explained by the macro economic factors. The change in worker attitudes is another hard to ascertain trend. The exact causes for the increased rejection of traditional legitimate decisions are difficult to identify but increased levels of education, full employment, increased affluence, and modern social welfare provisions are generally cited as underlying the changes in worker attitudes (O.E.C.D., 1974(b)). If the current hierarchical organization structures with their differentiated material and psychological reward systems become less generally accepted, new organizational designs must be found which do have some necessary degree of legitimacy. In this context the participative design process (Emery and Emery, 1974) of new forms of work organization reflects the historical trend from unilateral to bilateral legitimization procedures in industrial relations. In a democratic society 'management's unilateral right to manage' becomes more and more an empty slogan. Any right that management has in a democratic society must depend on the consent of that society and in particular on the consent of those managed. This consent will depend on the extent to which unilateral management decisions are considered legitimate by the workers. Job redesign is possibly also a response to a decrease in legitimacy ascribed to unilateral management decisions in certain areas. Dufty suggests an increasing managerial acceptance of the idea 'that the only way for management to retain control is to share it' (Dufty, 1973, 86).

A final perspective from which job redesign and work democratization can be analyzed is the one suggested by Strauss and Rosenstein (1970). They argue that 'participation' is partly a symbolic reconciliation between contradictory managerial and union ideologies rather than an organizational solution to any real life problems. The start of the Norwegian Cooperation Project partly motivated by a desire of the NAF to stall on the introduction of a board representation system, provides some support for Strauss and Rosenstein's argument. The more recent job redesign projects are of a very concrete nature and a response to practical management problems. The relationship of these projects to industrial democracy is therefore indeed merely a symbolic one.

The quality of working life issue that currently dominates Norwegian trade union discussions is certainly not job redesign, but health and safety. A recent study (Karlsen, 1972*) of a representative sample of 2262 LO members found that of the respondents:

47% complained about noise levels at work
45% complained about strain and stress at work
39% complained about draught at work
37% complained about the speed of work
30% complained about unpleasant temperatures
25% complained about eczema
21% complained about uncomfortable air conditions[5]

An independent study by the AFI (Karlsen et al., 1974*) also reported noise and stress as the most common worker complaints. The latter study also found that companies with a weak union organization inside the plant had clearly inferior safety and health conditions than firms with a well developed shop floor union organization.

Strain and stress and the speed of work are problems that fall within the area of job redesign. It seems however that in union circles the issues with a clear physical nature, e.g. the dangers involved with the production of and working with certain new chemicals, are central. Health and safety issues dominated the 1974 congresses of the Iron and Metal Workers and the Chemical Industry Workers. Work democratization and job redesign were not mentioned at these congresses. It was argued in Chapter IV that the

5. The percentages indicate that the respondents in this study could choose more than one of the problem areas.

health and safety issues better fit the collective ethic of unionism. The analysis of the health dangers of certain chemicals and the avoidance of sources of eczema at work are issues which must be dealt with by specialists and can be handled in the representative organs. The problems of strain and stress, draught, speed of work, unpleasant temperatures etc. can however be attacked by a similar process as was presented earlier for job redesign. Worker participation and influence in the decision-making processes regarding possible improvements in these areas can take place closer to the shop floor. Starting such a participatory process whereby workers can influence and change their jobs and working environment is from an industrial democracy point of view more relevant than which issues are to be handled in such a process.

The current developments in Norway do not show a tendency in this direction. The general emphasis in dealing with all the issues of the physical working environment is upon the representative structures in the trade unions, without much direct involvement of the shop floor workers in the individual companies. This approach could lead to solutions which are not optimal from the point of view of local shop floor conditions. Some of the recent accomplishments in this area in Norway are: increased research into the harmful effects of certain chemicals, new regulations regarding the functions of company doctors, and intensified government inspection of health and safety conditions. These are of course very useful attainments but they do not eliminate the potential danger that the Norwegian trade unions are approaching some of these issues at too high a level in their organizations. With respect to job redesign it can be concluded that job redesign today (Fall, 1974) is not 'alive' within the Norwegian trade unions, at least not at the practical policy level.

The start of the Norwegian Cooperation Project was a function of a particular historical, socio-political, and economic national context. A late and balanced industrialization process had facilitated the growth of a stable industrial relations system in Norway. The Norwegian trade unions attained a high degree of organization, Kassalow (1974) estimated that about 65% of the Norwegian labor force belongs to a trade union, and their strong ties to the Labor Party resulted in a societal power position which is comparable to that of the employers' interests. The Labor Party represents and integrates the Norwegian working class in the power centers of the nation.

This socio-political context provided the background setting of an industrial democracy debate in the late 1950's and early 1960's. The labor movement demanded more industrial democracy but did not have its demands very well defined. The employers' organization was afraid of the possibility that a scheme providing for worker representation on the board of directors would be legally imposed on Norwegian companies. Thorsrud's intervention in which he advocated industrial democracy through job redesign was well received. In his proposals Thorsrud linked the notion of industrial democracy, with its roots in socialist thought, to the Tavistock ideas of increased individual learning through more worker autonomy and responsibility at the shop floor level. Both LO and NAF, obviously for different individual reasons, decided to support experiments in job redesign. A few years later the government also gave its financial support to the experiments.

The Norwegian experiments in job design show great similarity to the current developments in most industrialized countries under the labels of the humanization of work, and the quality of working life. The essence of these developments is the question whether or not through certain forms of job complication the highly simplified industrial and white collar jobs can be improved in terms of greater worker autonomy and job satisfaction while at least maintaining current levels of productivity and efficiency.

The support of the government and national labor and employers' organizations in Norway legitimized the job design notions of the researchers involved in the early experiments. Later experiments show that this national institutional support might be a necessary condition to start experimentation in an organized manner, however this support does not determine whether or not an individual experiment is successful in terms of starting a democratizing process within a company.

The initiative to start a job redesign experiment is predominantly a management initiative. Management reacts to particular problems which are often related to the difficulties in attracting, maintaining and disciplining the necessary company labor force. A stringent labor market is the underlying cause of many of these managerial problems in Norway. This results in the paradoxal situation where increased industrial democracy should be the outcome of a management initiated and controlled job redesign program. An unilateral management introduction of a new work organization at the shop floor, which is basically the method followed in job enrichment in the U.S., can not be defined as contributing to industrial democracy. The boundaries of this type of democracy are well indicated by the following quote from an U.S. worker involved in an organizational change project: 'You can make any decision as long as it agrees with management' (Quoted in Elden, 1974, 8). In this type of projects the four necessary conditions in order for job redesign to contribute to industrial democracy are not met.[6] The projects are generally successful in terms of increased productivity and increased job satisfaction. The number of Norwegian companies where further democratization took place is probably limited to 7, this despite the supportive institutional environment.

A considerable gap exists between the theories and strategies for organizational democratization as presented in the literature and the manner in which they are implemented. The managerial control of the organization's hierarchy makes democratization difficult in particular because job redesign is characteristically not defined by management in terms of democracy but in terms of lower total production cost. If the immediate management problem is solved no motivation remains on the initiating and controlling side to continue the change process. The local union generally perceives job redesign also as a tool to attain its traditional objectives. The job redesign strategies which potentially could alter the traditional principles of organizational control through hierarchy and technology are redefined by management and the local union as just another means to achieve their traditional goals. These goals for management are cost reduction, higher productivity, and maintaining its position of power; for the union these goals are higher wages, better working conditions, and securing a stronger position inside the enterprise. Job redesign, as a form of direct worker participation, is perceived by management as a form of democracy which is preferred over the more formalized and institutionalized forms of representation of the worker interest. This could be one possible reason why local unions generally have not yet defined job redesign and improvement of individual jobs as an autonomous union bargaining goal. The existing managerial prerogative in the direction and organization of work has not yet been radically challenged by the unions. This challenge is necessary if workers themselves are going to influence the design of their work to any significant extent.

The organizational realities described here do not preclude the possibility that redesigned jobs provide the workers with more intrinsic satisfaction. A more challenging job, more variety, and increased autonomy and responsibility are changes to be positively evaluated in themselves. The start of a continuous democratization process can hardly be expected given current organizational conditions. Democratization has taken place in individual departments of companies, however diffusion into the larger organization has seldom taken place. The experimental department usually remains a 'foreign body' in a larger organization operating under different organizational principles.

6. See Chapter 5, p. 100.

The main contribution to industrial democracy by Einar Thorsrud and his collaborators has been his advocacy and partial implementation of opening up the job redesign process itself to workers and their representatives. The process of change and the changes in job design which result, are of coordinate importance. The experiments in Norway have shown that workers initially may resist changes in their jobs. However, after having experienced the redesigned work organization, they do not want to return to the old situation. Changes in job design have, in all cases, been accompanied by concomittant changes in the wage rate and wage system. In the successful cases a shelter agreement, which guarantees certain management and worker rights, has been agreed upon between management and the union, while in a later phase of the experiments changes in the work-effort bargain were referred to collective bargaining. Most unions have been able to renegotiate the wage system as a result of the introduction of new forms of work organization. At the national level LO and the national unions have not been successful in integrating job design and work democratization into their daily policies.

Potentially work democratization through job redesign can fill the gap left by the existing representative approaches to increase industrial democracy. Their representative nature inherently restricts the direct impact of those approaches on the shop floor. Representation is no alternative to active shop floor participation. Work democratization through job design is an essential element in the package approach towards industrial democracy. The Cooperation Project has shown that in a rather restricted number of companies (7), job redesign indeed did contribute to industrial democracy as defined earlier. The Cooperation Project also contributed to refinements of the socio-technical model, to a deepening insight into organizational change processes, to the identification of the importance of the change process itself, and to a better understanding of the difficult role of the social scientist as consultant. In Norway the Project led to a sharp decline in the use of time and motion studies, stimulated the introduction of fixed wage systems with predominantly small group bonuses and initiated the start of organizational change projects in the educational system and the important shipping industry. The Project also triggered experiments in Sweden (e.g. Volvo and Saab-Scania) and Denmark.[7]

7. For the developments in Sweden see Agervold (1972), Lindestad and Norstedt (1972), and Karlsson (1972). The Danish projects are well described in Agersnap et al. (1974) and in Thomsen and Olsen (1974). For an optimistic report on most European developments in this area see Jenkins (1973).

The complexity of the Norwegian Cooperation Project makes a simple concluding evaluation impossible. The developments as they present themselves today are ambiguous. The question whether or not job redesign has contributed to industrial democracy is difficult to answer. On the whole the Norwegian experience is not too positive from an industrial democracy perspective. On the other hand a rather small number of companies has progressed in a direction which seems to support the underlying theoretical notions of Einar Thorsrud and his collaborators. This ambivalence could be substantially reduced if the parties involved – employers, unions, workers, and researchers – make their objectives more explicit. The resulting clarity will facilitate the understanding of similar organizational change projects. It will also clarify whether or not the social scientist plays a 'democratizing' or merely a 'cost reducing – productivity enhancing' role.[8]

It is sometimes argued that the Norwegian experiments are not very relevant to the United States and other industrialized countries because of the distinct differences in the socio-political and economic environments. Despite this distinct context the actual changes in job design attained in a number of Norwegian firms do have general significance. In addition the number of other 'special cases' in Scandinavia, the rest of Western Europe, Australia, and the U.S. is steadily growing. Jenkins refutes the criticisms against work democratization based upon the 'special case' argument in the following manner:

'I have had it pointed out to me that the Kibbutzim in Israel are special because of ideology (or poverty, or because the country is at war): that Yugoslavia is special because it is Communist (or underdeveloped, or in conflict with the Soviet Union); that West Germany is special because of the unusual conditions under which codetermination was introduced; that Texas Instruments is special because it is a technologically advanced company; that Orrefors Glas is special because it is in a craft industry and thus technologically backward; that Procter and Gamble is special because it is a large company; that Nobø is special because it is a small company; that anyway the whole Scandinavian experience is special because everybody knows Scandinavians are 'different'; that Monsanto is special because it is capital-intensive; that R. G. Barry is special because it is labor intensive; and so on'. (Jenkins, 1973, 286).

Jenkins is obviously comparing quite different things with each other in this quote, however in a certain sense he is correct that any company or country is special. Today there exists a growing number of somewhat vaguely defined experiments in industrial democracy. Most of them are very modest in their impact, but it seems that more democratic forms of work organization have

8. Thorsrud's thesis is that these two roles are by no means mutually exclusive.

been developed under a wide variety of conditions (H.E.W., 1973, 188-201; Jenkins, 1973 and 1974). This study is an indication of a serious lack of hard data with respect to many of these experiments and the ambiguous relationship between job redesign and industrial democracy. Evidence is lacking not only in the area of the traditional economic and efficiency criteria, but also whether or not these changes contribute to industrial democracy. The earlier presented definition of industrial democracy could be used in operationalizing industrial democracy for the purposes of future evaluation studies. But, also in this area of lacking empirical evidence, Maslow's (1970, 149) 'If we wait for conventionally reliable data, we should have to wait forever' applies.

The implementation of the new *job design principles*, which does not necessarily mean organizational democratization, will only be accelerated if at least one of the following developments takes place:

1. A manifest 'proof' that the new job design principles will substantially increase efficiency and/or productivity. The information so far indicates a positive relationship between these criteria and redesigned jobs;[9] however, detailed information about the actual changes which took place and their impact on efficiency and productivity is still lacking. If this positive relation is 'proven' management will have a strong incentive to become active in the area of job design.
2. Strict enforcement of social and psychological criteria in the evaluation of enterprises and managers. Despite recent progress in operationalizing social indicators (see e.g. Lawler, 1972; I.R.R.A., 1973, 99-119; O.E.C.D., 1973(b); O.E.C.D., 1974(a)) they do not yet have any significant impact on practical company decision making.

'In spite of all lip service paid to social and psychological criteria, in practical life, the economic and technical criteria dominate. The reason for this is not only that these two sets of criteria are still critical ones for organizations, but also that little is done to make other criteria practicable, i.e. the need to provide conditions for learning,, participation in decision-making, conditions for cooperation and social support, etc.' (Thorsrud, 1974, 67).

Only by making use of such criteria mandatory at the company level will job redesign occur. A required human resource accounting system for- in stance would naturally lead to increased attention to issues like training, education, and learning. As long as management is solely rewarded on

9. Kuipers (1972*) in an evaluation study of Dutch job redesign experiments talks about a 'marked' success of the changes in terms of efficiency and productivity.

the basis of financial performance we cannot expect a sharp increase in attention to these new criteria. At the company level today it is not yet true that 'objectives of efficiency and economic growth are losing their exclusive primacy' (Seashore, 1974, 133), neither are we now 'in the after days of classic patterns of efficiency behavior . . .' (Van der Does, 1972, 53).

3. Demands from workers for changes at the shop floor. These demands can either be formulated through collective bargaining or be expressed in behavior like absenteeism and turnover, or, as is the case in Norway and Sweden, by increased workers' refusal to work in companies which offer unattractive jobs.

The possible occurrence of one of these developments will not automatically lead to increased industrial democracy. This will be determined by the extent to which workers participate and influence the job redesign process, which will be the expected management response to any of these above posited developments.

It was argued here that the introduction of changes in job redesign can best be controlled by collective bargaining. In collective bargaining the workers' interests are looked after under fairly equal power conditions. Work democratization is one possible method to increase industrial democracy. The other methods presented in the 'Package Approach' need to be supplemented by work democratization in order to provide increased opportunities for direct participation and autonomy at the shop floor. With respect to developments in work democratization in Norway, it seems that further shop floor democratization in the near future can only be expected to occur as a possible external effect on management's efforts to increase productivity and maintain a stable labor force. It will depend on the union local and shop stewards whether these management efforts will be controlled in such a manner that work democratization can take place. Karlsson is rather pessimistic about these chances, he concludes from Swedish experiments that 'as long as the authoritarian firm makes a normal or reasonable profit the people in power prefer to maintain the established order rather than to create a more efficient but democratic organization' (Karlsson, 1973, 51).

Full industrial democracy and in particularly a full participatory enterprise are most likely utopian visions. This does not mean however that we should not attempt to approach them as closely as possible. Work democratization through job redesign certainly is one means to attain an increased measure of participatory democracy in our modern enterprises.

References in English

Adizes, I., *Industrial Democracy: Yugoslav Style*. New York: The Free Press, 1971.

Agersnap, F., F. Junge, A. Westenholtz, P. Møldrup and L. Brinch, Danish experiments with new forms of cooperation on the shop floor. *Personnel Review*, 1974, 3(3), 34-50.

Agervold, M., Swedish experiments in democracy at work. Paper presented at the International Conference on the Quality of Working Life. Arden House, New York, September 1972.

Argyris, C., The Individual and Organization: An Empirical Test. *Administrative Science Quarterly*, 1959, 4, 145-167.

Argyris, C., Personality and Organization Theory Revisted. *Administrative Science Quarterly*, 1973, 18, 141-167.

Aspengren, T., Industrial Democracy. Speech delivered at the Nordic Labor Congress in Stockholm, June 15-17, 1973.

Aspengren, T., What Do We Mean By Democracy in Industry? In C. Levinson (ed.), *Industry's Democratic Revolution*. London: Allen and Unwin, 1974.

Barbash, J., Trade Unionism and The General Interest: A Theory of Positive Public Policy Toward Labor. *Wisconsin Law Review*, 1970, 4, 1134-1144.

Barbash, J., Elements of Industrial Relations. Madison: University of Wisconsin (mimeograph), 1971.

Barbash, J., The Tensions of Work. *Dissent*, Winter 1972, 240-248.

Barbash, J., Job Satisfaction Attitude Surveys. Paris: O.E.C.D., 1974(a).

Barbash, J., Trade Unions, More and The Humanization of Work or is There More to More Than More? Madison: University of Wisconsin (mimeograph), 1974(b).

Barbash, J., *Work in a Changing Industrial Society*. Final report of an O.E.C.D. Conference with the same name. Paris: O.E.C.D., 1975.

Berle, A. and G. Means, *The Modern Corporation and Private Property*. New York: Mcmillan, 1934.

Blanpain, R., The Influence of Labour on Management Decision Making: A Comparative Legal Survey. *Industrial Law Journal*, March 1974, 5-19.

Blauner, R., *Alienation and Freedom*. Chicago: Chicago University Press, 1964.

Bluestone, I., The Next Step Towards Industrial Democracy. Detroit: U.A.W. paper, 1972(a).

Bluestone, I., Democratizing the Work Place. Detroit: U.A.W. paper, 1972(b).

Bluestone, I., The System of Work – A New Look Needed. Detroit: U.A.W. paper, 1972(c).

Blumberg, P., *Industrial Democracy: The Sociology of Participation*. London: Constable, 1968.

Bolweg, J., An Old Road Towards Industrial Democracy Finally Feasible? Madison: University of Wisconsin (mimeograph), 1973.

Bolweg, J. and M. Weisz, Introduction. In: *Work in a Changing Industrial Society*. Paris: O.E.C.D., 1974, 8-20.

Broekhoven, R. V., Evaluation of Business Economic Effects of Autonomous Task-Oriented Production Groups. Eindhoven: Philips Internal Document, 1973.

Broekmeyer, M. J. (ed.), *Yugoslav Workers' Self-Management*. Dordrecht (Holland): Reidel, 1970.

Brooks, T. R., Job Satisfaction: An Elusive Goal. *AFL-CIO Federationist*, 1972, 79 (10), 1-7.

Bull, E., The Norwegian Trade-Union Movement. Brussels: I.C.F.T.U., 1956.

Burbidge, J. J., The Effect of Group Production Methods on Workers' Participation in Decisions. Paper presented at the I.L.O. Symposium on Workers' Participation. Oslo: August, 1974.

Cherns, A. B., Better Working Lives – A Social Scientist's View. *Occupational Psychology*, 1973, 14, 23–28.

Cherns, A. B. and L. E. Davis, Assessment of the State of the Art. In A. B. Cherns and L. E. Davis (eds.), *The Quality of Working Life*. New York: Free Press, 1975.

Clark, P. A., *Organizational Design*. London: Tavistock, 1972.

Clegg, H. A., *A New Approach to Industrial Democracy*. Oxford: Blackwell, 1960.

Cole, G. D. H., *The Case for Industrial Partnership*. London: Mcmillan, 1957.

Daniel, W. W., *Beyond the Wage Bargain*. London: MacDonald, 1970.

Daniel, W. W., What Interests a Worker? *New Society*, March 23, 1972, 083-586.

Daniel, W. W. and N. McIntosh, *The Right to Manage?* London: MacDonald, 1972.

Davis, L. E., R. R. Canter and J. Hoffman, Current Job Design Criteria. In L. E. Davis and J. C. Taylor (eds.), *Design of Jobs*. Penguin Books, 1972.

Davis, L. E. and J. C. Taylor (eds.), *Design of Jobs*. Middlesex: Penguin, 1972.

Delamotte, Y., *The Social Partners Face the Problem of Productivity and Employment*. Paris: O.E.C.D., 1971.

Delamotte, Y. and L. Walker, Humanization of Work and the Quality of Working Life – Trends and Issues. *I.I.L.S. Bulletin*, 1974, 11, 3-14.

Den Hertog, J. F. and W. H. Kerkhoff, Evaluation of the Social Psychological Effects of Autonomous Task-Oriented Production Groups. Eindhoven: Philips internal document, 1973.

Derber, M., *The American Idea of Industrial Democracy, 1865-1965*. Urbana (Ill.): University of Illinois Press, 1970.

Dorfman, H., *Labor Relations in Norway*. Oslo: International Social Policy, 1966.

Dronkers, P. L., Labour/Management Cooperation for Productivity and Job Satisfaction. Paris: O.E.C.D. Seminar on Labour/Management Cooperation in the Enterprise, 1972.

Dubin, R. (ed.), *The Handbook of Work, Organization, and Society*. Chicago: Rand McNally, 1976 (forthcoming).

Duckles, R. and J. Lyle, Work Improvement Program Harman International. Progress report. Bolivar (Tenn.): 1974.

Dufty, N. F., *Changes in Labour-Management Relations in the Enterprise*. Paris: O.E.C.D., 1973.

Elden, M., The Anatomy of Autonomy: A View From the Inside. Oslo: AFI, 1974.

Elden, M. and H. Engelstad, A Preliminary Evaluation of Experimental Outcomes Based on Interviews with Hunsfos Workers in 1970. Oslo: AFI, 1973.

Emery, F. E., Democratization of the Work Place. *Manpower and Applied Psychology*, 1966, 1, 118-129.

Emery, F. E. and M. Emery, Participative Design, Oslo: AFI, 1974.

Emery, F. E. and E. Thorsrud, A New Look at Industrial Democracy. Paper presented at the International Congress of Applied Psychology. Ljubljana, August, 1964.

Emery, F. E. and E. Thorsrud, *Form and Content in Industrial Democracy*. London: Tavistock, 1969.

Emery, F. E. and E. C. Trist, The Causal Texture of Organizational Environments. *Human Relations*, 1965, 18, 21-32.

Engelstad, P., Socio-technical Approach to Problems of Process Control. In L. Davis and J. C. Taylor (eds.), *Design of Jobs*. Middlesex: Penguin, 1972.

European Trade Union Confederation (ETUC), *Action Programme*. Brussels: ETUC, 1974.

Fein, M., The Real Needs and Goals of Blue Collar Workers. *The Conference Board Record*, February 1973(a), 26-33.

Fein, M., The Myth of Job Enrichment. *The Humanist*, 1973(b), XXXIII(5), 30-33.

Fein, M., Job Enrichment: A Revaluation. *Sloan Management Review*, 1974, 15(2), 69-88.

Filley, A. C. and R. J. House, *Managerial Process and Organizational Behavior*. Glenview: Scott, Foreman and Company, 1969.

Fisher, M., *Measurement of Labour Disputes and Their Economic Effects*. Paris: O.E.C.D., 1973.

Flanagan, R. J., G. Strauss and L. Ulman, Worker Discontent and Workplace Behavior. *Industrial Relations*, 1974, 13(2), 101-123.

Form, W., Job Versus Political Unionism: A Cross-national Comparison. *Industrial Relations*, 1973, 12(2), 224-238.

Fox, A., *A Sociology of Work in Industry*. London: Mcmillan, 1971.

Furstenberg, F., Worker's Participation in Management in the Federal Republic of Germany. *I.L.L.S. Bulletin*, 1969, 6, 94-148.

Galbraith, J. K., *The New Industrial State*. New York: Signet, 1968.

Galenson, W. (ed.), *Comparative Labor Movements*. Englewood Cliffs: Prentice Hall, 1952.

Gide, C. and C. Rist, *A History of Economic Doctrines*. New York: Heath, 1909.

Goldthorpe, J. H., D. Lockwood, F. Bechhofer and J. Platt, *The Affluent Worker in the Class Structure*. Cambridge: University Press, 1969.

Gorz, A., *Strategy for Labor*. Boston: Beacon Press, 1968.

Gulowsen, J., A Measure of Work-Group Autonomy. In L. Davis and J. C. Taylor (eds.), *Design of Jobs*. Middlesex: Penguin, 1972.

Gustavsen, B., Autonomous Groups and Employee Participation in Norway. Paper presented at I.L.O. Symposium on Workers' Participation. Oslo: August, 1974.

Gyllenhammar, R., Changing Work Organization at Volvo. *Industrial Participation*, Spring 1974, No. 554, 5-10.

Hackman, J. R. and E. E. Lawler, Employee Reactions to Job Characteristics. *Journal of Applied Psychology*, 1971, 55, 259-286.

Hage, J. and M. Aiken, *Social Change in Complex Organizations*. New York: Random House, 1970.

Halverson, T., Democracy in Industry. Oslo: LO, 1971.

Herbst, P. G., *Autonomous Group Functioning*. London: Tavistock, 1962.

Herbst, P. G., Socio-technical Design: Strategies in Multi-disciplinary Research. Oslo: AFI, 1970.

Herbst, P. G., Socio-technical Design: Strategies in Multi-disciplinary Research. London: Tavistock, 1974(a).

Herbst, P. G., Some Reflections on the Work Democratization Project. Oslo: AFI, 1974(b).

Herbst, P. G., Types of Research in the Social Sciences. Oslo: AFI, 1974(c).

Herzberg, F., B. Mausner and B. Snyderman, *The Motivation to Work*. New York: Wiley, 1959.

H.E.W. Task Force Report on *Work in America*. Cambridge: MIT Press, 1973.
Holter, H., Attitudes Towards Employee Participation in Company Decision Making Processes. *Human Relations*, 1965, 18, 291-321.
Hulin, C. L. and M. R. Blook, Job Enlargement, Individual Differences and Worker Responses. *Psychological Bulletin*, 1968, 69, 41-55.
Hunnius, G., G. D. Garson and J. Case (eds.), *Workers' Control*, New York: Random House, 1973.
I.L.O., *Collective Bargaining in Industrialized Market Economies*. Geneva: I.L.O., 1974(a).
I.L.O., Background paper for the 1974 Oslo Symposium on Workers' Participation in Decisions Within Undertakings. Geneva: I.L.O., 1974(b).
I.R.R.A., *Proceedings of the Twenty-Fifth Anniversary Meeting*. Madison: IRRA, 1973.
Jenkins, D., *Job Power: Blue and White Collar Democracy*. New York: Double Day, 1973.
Jenkins, D., *Industrial Democracy in Europe*. Geneva: Business International, 1974.
Karlsen, J. I., A monography on the Norwegian Industrial Democracy Project. Oslo: AFI, 1972.
Karlsson, L. E., Experiences in Employee Participation in Sweden: 1969-1972. Stockholm: Socialhögskolan (mimeograph), 1973.
Kassalow, E. M., *Trade Unions and Industrial Relations: An International Comparison*. New York: Random House, 1969.
Kassalow, E. M., Conflict and Cooperation in Europe's Industrial Relations. *Industrial Relations*, 1974, 13, 156-163.
Kohn, M. and C. Schooler, Occupational Experience and Psychological Functioning: An Assessment of Reciprocal Effects. *American Sociological Review*, 1973, 38, 97-118.
Lafferty, W. W., *Economic Development and the Response of Labor in Scandinavia*. Oslo: Universitetsforlaget, 1971.
Larsen, R., Autonomous Groups and Employee Participation in Norway. Paper presented at the I.L.O. Symposium on Workers' Participation. Oslo: August, 1974.
Larsen, R. and K. Hansen, Norway. Seminar on Labor/Management Cooperation in the Enterprise. Paris: O.E.C.D., 1972.
Lawler, E. E., Job Design and Employee Motivation. *Personnel Psychology*, 1969, 22, 426-435.
Lawler, E. E., Measuring the Quality of Working Life: The Why and How of it All. Ann Harbor: Institute for Social Research (mimeograph), 1972.
Likert, R., *New Patterns of Management*. New York: McGraw-Hill, 1961.
Lindestad, H. and J. Norstedt, *Autonomous Groups and Payment by Result*. Stockholm: S.A.F., 1973.
Lindsay, A. D., *The Modern Democratic State*. New York: Oxford University Press, 1962.
L.O., *Norwegian Federation of Trade unions*. Oslo: LO, 1971.
L.O., (Sweden) Industrial Democracy. Programme adopted by the 1971 L.O. Congress. Stockholm: L.O., 1972.
Martin, P. G., Party Strategies and Social Change: The Norwegian Labor Party. Unpublished Ph.D. Dissertation, Yale University: 1972.
Maslow, A., *Motivation and Personality*. New York: Harper and Row, 1970.
McGregor, D., *The Human Side of Enterprise*. New York: McGraw-Hill, 1960.
Meissner, M., The Long Arm of the Job: A Study of Work and Leisure. *Industrial Relations*, 1971, 10, 239-260.
Michels, R., *Political Parties*. Glencoe: Free Press, 1958.
Mulder, M., Power Equalization Through Participation? *Administrative Science Quarterly*, 1971, 16, 31-39.
Norstedt, J. P. and S. Aguren, *The Saab-Scania Report*. Stockholm: S.A.F., 1973.
O.E.C.D., *Absenteeism and Staff Turnover*. Report on a meeting of management experts. Paris: O.E.C.D., 1973(a).

O.E.C.D., *List of Social Concerns Common to Most O.E.C.D. Countries.* Paris: O.E.C.D., 1973(b).
O.E.C.D., *Social Indicators the O.E.C.D. Experience.* Paris: O.E.C.D., 1974(a).
O.E.C.D., *Work In a Changing Industrial Society.* Paris: O.E.C.D., 1974(b).
Pateman, C., *Participation and Democratic Theory.* London: Cambridge University Press, 1970.
Parker, S., *The Future of Work and Leisure.* London: Paladin, 1972.
Perlman, S., *The Theory of the Labor Movement.* New York: Mcmillan, 1928.
Perrow, C., A Framework for the Comparative Analysis of Organizations. *American Sociological Review,* 1967, 32, 194-208.
Perrow, C., *Complex Organizations.* Glenview: Scott, Foresman, 1972.
Phillips, D., *Abandoning Method.* San Francisco: Jossey-Bass, 1973.
Qvale, T. U., Strategies for Change: Some Norwegian Experiences in Industrial Participation. Paper presented to a conference of the British Sociological Association on Participation and Democracy. London: March, 1973(a).
Qvale, T. U., Participation and Conflict. Paper presented at the Third World Congress of the International Industrial Relations Association. London: September, 1973(b).
Rice, A. K., *Productivity and Social Organization: The Ahmedabad Experiment.* London: Tavistock, 1958.
Roethlisberger, F. J. and W. J. Dickson, *Management and the Worker.* Cambridge: Harvard University Press, 1939.
Sapulkas, A., Work Democracy Tested at Scandinavian Plants. *New York Times,* November 11, 1974(a).
Sapulkas, A., Swedish Autoplant Drops Assembly-line. *New York Times,* November 12, 1974(b).
Sapulkas, A., Reform of Work: Move for Creative Jobs Stirs Debate. *New York Times,* November 13, 1974(c).
Schregle, J., Labor Relations in Western Europe: Some Topical Issues. *International Labour Review,* 1974, 109(1), 1-22.
Seashore, S., Work and the Future. In: *Work in a Changing Industrial Society.* Paris: O.E.C.D., 1974, 121-134.
Selznick, P., *Law, Society and Industrial Justice.* New York: Russell Sage, 1969.
Shaw, M. E., *Group Dynamics: The Psychology of Small Group Behavior.* New York: McGraw-Hill, 1971.
Sheppard, H. L. and N. Q. Herrick, *Where Have All the Robots Gone?* New York: Free Press, 1972.
Silverman, D., *The Theory or Organizations.* London: Heineman, 1970.
Skard, Ø., General Evaluation of the Norwegian Experiments with Partly Autonomous Groups. Oslo: N.A.F. paper, 1973.
Strauss, G. and E. Rosenstein, Workers' Participation: A Critical View. *Industrial Relations,* 1970, 9, 197-214.
Sturmthal, A., *Workers' Councils.* Cambridge: Harvard University Press, 1964.
Sturmthal, A., Workers' Participation in Management: A Review of United States Experience. *I.I.L.S. Bulletin,* 1969, 6, 149-186.
Supek, R., Problems and Perspectives of Workers' Self-management in Yugoslavia. In M. Broekmeyer (ed.), *Yugoslav Workers' Self-Management.* Dordrecht (Holland): Reidel, 1970, 216-241.
Taylor, F. W., *The Principles of Scientific Management.* New York: Harper, 1923.
Taylor, J. C., *The Quality of Working Life, An Annotated Bibliography.* Los Angeles: University of California, 1972.
Teulings, A., Representation of Workers' Interest and Consultation in the Dutch Works Council. *Sociologia Neerlandica,* 1970, 5, 80-102.

Thomsen, S. V. and E. E. Olsen, *Experiments in Industrial Cooperation*. Copenhagen: Federation of Danish Mechanical Engineering and Metalworking Industries, 1974.

Thorsrud, E., A Strategy for Research and Social Change in Industry: A Report on the Industrial Democracy Project in Norway. *Social Science Information*, 1970, 9(5), 65-90.

Thorsrud, E., Policy Making as a Learning Process. In A. B. Cherns et al. (eds.), *Social Science and Government*. London: Tavistock, 1971, 39-66.

Thorsrud, E., Workers' Participation in Management in Norway. Oslo: AFI paper, 1972(a).

Thorsrud, E., The Organization of Industry and Trade Unions. In R. Hayne (ed.), *Europe Tomorrow*. London: Collins, 1972(b), 289-309.

Thorsrud, E., The Industrial Democracy Project in Norway. Oslo: AFI, 1973. Forthcoming in R. Dubin, (ed.), *The Handbook of Work, Organization, and Society*. Chicago: Rand McNally.

Thorsrud, E., Changes in Work Organization and Managerial Roles. In: *Work in a Changing Industrial Society*. Paris: O.E.C.D., 1974, 65-82.

Tinbergen, J., Does Self-management Approach the Optimum. In M. Broekmeyer (ed.), *Yugoslav Workers' Self-management*. Dordrecht (Holland): Reidel, 1970, 117-127.

Trist, E. L. and K. W. Banforth, Some Social and Psychological Consequences of the Long-wall Method of Goal-getting. *Human Relations*, 1951, 4, 3-38.

Trist, E. L., G. W. Higgin, H. Murray and A. B. Pollock, *Organizational Choice*. London: Tavistock, 1963.

Turner, A. M. and P. Lawrence, *Industrial Jobs and the Worker*. Cambridge: Harvard University Press, 1965.

U.S. Department of Labor, Job Satisfaction is There a Trend? Manpower Research monograph No. 30, 1974.

Van der Does de Willebois, J. L., On the Quality of Working Life. In W. Albeda (ed.), *Participation in Management*. Rotterdam, University Press, 1973.

Wachtel, H. M., *Workers' Management and Workers' Wages in Yugoslavia*. Ithaca: Cronell University Press, 1973.

Walker, K. F., *Industrial Democracy*. London: Times Newspapers, 1970.

Walker, K. F., Workers' Participation in Management – Problems, Practice and Prospects. *I.L.L.S. Bulletin*, 1975, 12, 3-35.

Walker, K. F. and L. Greyfie de Bellecombe, Workers' Participation in Management. *I.I.L.S. Bulletin*, 1967, 2, 67-125.

Webbs, S. and B. Webb, *Industrial Democracy*. London: Longmans, 1902.

Weick, K. E., *The Social Psychology of Organizing*. Reading: Addison – Wesley, 1969.

Wilensky, H., Work Careers and Social Integration. *International Social Science Journal*, 1960, 12, 543-574.

Wilkinson, A., *A Survey of Some Western European Eexperiments in Motivation*. Enfield U.K.: Institute of Work Study Practioners, 1970.

Wilpert, B., Research on Industrial Democracy: The German Case. West Berlin: International Institute of Management, 1973.

Winpisinger, W., Job Satisfaction: A Union Response. *AFL-CIO Federationist*, 1973, 80 (2), 3-10.

Woodcock, L., U.S.A. In C. Levinson (ed.), *Industry's Democratic Revolution*. London: Allen and Unwin, 1974.

Zupanov, J., Two Patterns of Conflict Management in Industry. *Industrial Relations*, 1973, 12(2), 213-223.

Non-English references

Anker-Ording, A., *Bedrift demokrati*. Oslo: Universitetsforlaget, 1965.

Arbeidspsykologisk Institutt, *Prosjekter 1964-72*. Oslo: AFI, 1973.

Bartveit, H., Socio-Teknisk forskning som rasjonalisering. Bergen: Sociologisk Institutt, 1973.

Blume, U., Zehn Jahre Mitbestimmung. In E. Sothoff, D. Blume and H. Duvernell (eds.), *Zwischenbilanz der Mitbestimmung*. Tübingen: Mohr, 1962.

Cieslak, W., Zukunft der Gewerkschaften. In *Qualität des Lebens No. 9*. Frankfurt: Europäische Verlagsanstalt, 1972.

Engelstad, P., *Teknologi og sosial forandring pa arbeidsplassen*. Oslo: Tanum, 1970.

Gulowsen, J., *Selvstyrte Arbeidsgrupper*. Oslo: Tanum, 1971.

Gulowsen, J., *Bedriftsdemokrati ved Norsk Hydro?* Oslo: AFI, 1974.

Gulowsen, J., J. I. Karlsen, S. Seierstad and T. U. Qvale, Faktorer som pavirker framdrift of stagnasjon i utviklingen av selvstyre og learing blant de ansatte i forsøkavdelingen. Oslo: AFI, 1973.

Gustavsen, B., *Industristyret*. Oslo: Tanum, 1972.

Hammarstrøm, O., *Handbok i företagsdemokrati för löntagare*. Stockholm: Prisma, 1974.

Herbst, P. G., *Demokratiserings prosessen i arbeidslivet*. Oslo: Universitetsforlaget, 1971.

Jarlsby, T. R., For passiv holding i N.A.F. og L.O. til systemet med delvis selvstyrte grupper. *Arbeidsgivern*, 1973, 1, 10-13.

Karlsen, J. E., *Arbeidsmiljo og arbeidsskader*. Oslo: L.O., 1972.

Karlsen, J. I. et al., *Arbeidsmiljo og vernearbeid*. Oslo: AFI, 1974.

Kokkvold, A., Utfordringen til Norsk Arbeiderbewegelse. *Socialistisk Perspektiv*, 1968, 4, 30-34.

Kuipers, J. H., *Verantwoordelijkheidsverruiming in de directe werksituatie*. Amsterdam: Vrije Universiteit, 1972.

Landsradet for Produktsjonutvalg, *Forslags Virksomheten*. Oslo: 1954.

Lange, K., Hverdagens industrielle demokrati. *Sosialistisk Perspektiv*, 1969, 2, 1-6.

L.O. - N.A.F., *Hovedevtalen av 1974*. Oslo: LO, 1974.

Mulder, M., *Het spel om de macht*. Meppel: Boom, 1972.

N.A.F., *Samarbeide i arbeidslivet*. Oslo: NAF-NIF, 1965.

Ødegaard, L. A., Sosio-teknisk analyse og organisasjonsutforming. *Tiddsskrift for Samfunnsforskning*, 1969, 10, 279-296.

Peper, A. and J. J. Ramondt, *Arbeidsverhouding en industriële democratie in Noorwegen*. Den Haag, COP/SER, 1973.

Philips' Centrale Ondernemingsraad, *Werkstructurering gezien van onderaf*. Eindhoven: Philips, 1973.

Qvale, T. U., Menneskelige ressurser og medevirkning i lageravelinger. Oslo: AFI, 1974.

Ramondt, J., Bedrijfsdemocratisering zonder arbeiders. Alphen aan den Rijn: Samson, 1974.
Riste,Ø., Demokratiseringsprosessen i andre former. Oslo: AFI, 1973(a).
Riste,Ø., Produksjonutvalgene. Oslo: AFI, 1973(b).
Samarbeidsradet, *Et ord med i laget*. Oslo: 1972.
Samarbeidsradet, *Vurdering av Samarbeidsprosjektets spredningsfase*. Oslo: 1973.
Selvig, K., Interview in *Informasjon om Samarbeidsforsøk*, 1972, 2, 4-7.
Skard, Ø., Demokratiseringsprosessen i bedriftslivet – Hvordan fa det til a virke? Oslo: N.A.F. peper, 1973.
Stenersen, O., Om opprettelsen og utviklingen av produksjonutvalg i norsk industri. Oslo: Hovedfagsoppgave in historie, 1972.
Thorsrud, E. and F. E. Emery, *Mot en ny bedriftsorganisasjon*. Oslo: Tanum, 1970.
Van Zuthem, H. J. *Inleiding in de economische sociologie*. Amsterdam: De Bussy, 1973.
Vilmar, F. (ed.), *Menschenwurde im Betrieb*. Hamburg: Rowohlt, 1973.

The following Norwegian newspapers were regularly consulted: *Aftenposten*, *Arbeiderbladet*, and *Fri Fagbewegelse*.

Appendix

Project shelter agreement of a Norwegian company

1. Shielding

The project shall take place at the repair department for trucks at ... The project shall not include ... The project area includes the repair hall for trucks, including the greasing ramp, the gangway, the motor room, tool shed, diesel room with office, expedition, planning room and conference room (information center).

All measures and changes in connection with the experiment in the project area *only apply* to this area and shall not have any influence on other departments.

2. Project leadership

The project is led by a committee hereafter called the working committee. This committee is responsible to the local union and management in directing the project. The working committee shall consist of representatives from the local union and management. It shall have four members, two from each partner in the company.

3. Termination

Both partners in the project, local union and management, can whenever they wish and without special reasons terminate this project agreement. Work will thereafter be performed under the circumstances that existed before the start of the project.

4. Wages

The partners agree that wage developments shall not be disrupted by factors related to the project, that is to say that wage developments in the project area shall not differ from those which are common for identical work in other departments. Wage increases which could result from increases in productivity under the project fall outside the scope of the foregoing stipulation.

5. Productivity

The partners agree that they shall not accept a reduction in productivity as a result of the project. Productivity will be monitored continuously and computed over periods of at least three months.

6. Duration

This project agreement applies one year from the date that the project is started. Otherwise the regular agreement applies.

Project shelter agreement U.S. company (Union U.A.W.)

The purpose of the joint management-labor *Work Improvement Program* is to make work better and more satisfying for all employees, salaried and hourly, while maintaining the necessary productivity for job security.

The purpose is not to increase productivity. If increased productivity is a by-product of the program, ways of rewarding the employees for increased productivity will become legitimate matters for inclusion in the program.

A *Review Committee* will meet monthly to hear reports on and review the activities of the Work Improvement Program. The Review Committee will consist of the members of the Bargaining Committee of the local union and three people designated by management.

A *Working Committee* will plan and coordinate the day-to-day work improvement program. The membership of the Working Committee will be: The President of the union local, four members of the union selected by the President of the union local, subject to the review of the Review Committee, and five people designated by management. One member of the Bargaining Committee will attend each Working Committee meeting.

No worker will lose his job, pay, or seniority as a result of a work improvement experiment conducted in the plant, whether he is a participant in the experiment or not.

Participation in an experiment in the Work Improvement Program is voluntary. No one will be forced to participate.

Trying new ideas requires extra flexibility on everyone's part. The union and the company will both cooperate in trying out new ideas in experimental groups, giving new ways of doing things a chance to prove themselves. This does not mean that either party relinquishes its contractual rights. Termination of the program by either party will require 30 days notice.